12

CHOICES...

THAT LEAD TO YOUR SUCCESS

DAVID COTTRELL

12 Choices...
That Lead to Your Success

Inquiries regarding permission for use of the material contained in this book should be addressed to:

CornerStone Leadership Institute
P.O. Box 764087
Dallas, TX 75376
888.789.LEAD

Printed in the United States of America
ISBN: 0-9762528-1-3

Credits
Design, art direction, and production   Melissa Monogue, Back Porch Creative, Plano, TX
info@BackPorchCreative.com

Choice

1. The act of **selection** after consideration.
2. The **power** or liberty of choosing.

Success

1. The **achievement** of something desired.
2. The gaining of **prosperity**.

"The person who wakes up and finds himself
a success hasn't been asleep."
~ Wilson Mizner, U.S. dramatist ~

How to Get the Most Out of This Book!

 Read with a highlighter in your hand. Mark key words or phrases that pertain to your personal situation.

 Read it once all the way through and then read two chapters a day for a week. Evaluate your current situation and develop a personal plan to improve your success in both of the choices read each day.

 When you complete this book, teach the contents to someone else. Everybody wins when you teach others. Give your knowledge away and you will become more knowledgeable.

 Make the choice to pay the price of success and enjoy the ride!

Table of Contents

Table of Contents

Introduction:
The Choices for Success   7

Part One: **The Character Choices ...**
         the foundation of success

1. The no-victim choice ... don't let your past eat your future.   15
2. The commitment choice ... passionate enough to succeed.   23
3. The values choice ... choosing the right enemies.   33
4. The integrity choice ... doing the right thing.   41

Part Two: **The Action Choices ...**
         the movement toward success

5. The do-something choice ... don't vacation on Someday Isle.   51
6. The persistence choice ... learning from failure.   63
7. The attitude choice ... the enthusiastic approach.   71
8. The adversity choice ... conquering difficult times.   83

Part Three: **The Investment Choices ...**
         the profit of success

9. The relationship choice ... connecting with success.   93
10. The criticism choice ... tough learning.   101
11. The reality choice ... facing truth.   109
12. The legacy choice ... your gift.   117

The Final Word:
Preparing for your special moment of success   128

Introduction
The Choices for Success

~

"You are free to choose, but the choices you make today
will determine what you will have, be and
do in the tomorrow of your life."
– Zig Ziglar

What do you need to do to be successful right now?

If you asked people in a typical organization that question, many would say success is a matter of being in the right place at the right time. Some would say successful people were just lucky – good fortune fell into their laps. Some may even attribute success to their ancestors – they inherited success.

Has anyone ever been successful entirely because of good luck? Maybe, but not likely! Luck, happenstance, being in the right place at the right time, and family inheritance all may help, of course, but the reality is that many people have been in the right place at the right time, had good fortune come their way, and were born into a wealthy family … yet they never experience success.

So what do you need to do to be successful right now?

Success is ultimately realized by people who make more right choices … and recover quickly from their bad choices.

Choices are directional … they lead us toward or away from the success that we are trying to achieve. Our personal and professional success depends on repeating good choices day in and day out … and avoid repeating bad choices.

Take a look at the successful people you know … in your office, your neighborhood, your city or your family. Without exception, their success has been created by their choices. It's not about luck, the conditions or even the guardian angels guiding their lives.

Now take a closer look at these successful people. They share some common traits, but – believe it or not – there is not an enormous difference between highly successful people and those not so successful.

For instance, do you think that the salesperson who earns $250,000 a year has five times the intellect or the ability of the salesperson earning $50,000 a year selling the same product in a similar territory? Of course not.

So what's the difference?

A major difference is that successful people make choices that others don't like to make. If you ask the successful people, they may tell you that they may not want to make those choices, either, but they also realize that there is often a greater purpose in choosing to do things they may not want to do.

Some choices that help create success are never seen by others. They are **character choices** known only to the person making them. These character choices include deciding not to be a victim, to be committed and passionate enough to succeed, choosing values, and making the integrity choice.

There are also **action choices** that move you toward success. Those choices include the do-something choice – moving beyond talk and getting things done; the persistence choice – when you stick to the objective long enough to win; the attitude choice – taking an enthusiastic approach to work and life; and the adversity choice – attacking and conquering difficult issues.

Then there are the **investment choices** through which you reap the profit of success. Those choices include investing in relationships, learning from criticism, being realistic about your strengths and weaknesses, and leaving a legacy that will live through generations.

This book, based on the experiences of many and the observations of many more, will provide insight into 12 choices others have made – and you can make – to enhance your chances for success in your career. The path we'll mark is not an easy one, but the sum total of these 12 choices creates a philosophy that not only allows you to make better decisions, but encourages success in every aspect of your life.

When you accept responsibility to make conscious choices for success, you seize the power that choices offer and stop being a hapless individual to which life happens. **With your choices, you take control of your success.**

THE CHALLENGE

The task of making good choices is a never-ending challenge … requiring plain hard work and diligence. We also get a lot of practice, because life requires that we choose between alternatives every hour of the day, every day of our lives.

Whether it's selecting one political candidate over another, filling an important position on the team, deciding how to deal with a difficult situation at work, or simply choosing a habit, such as pouring a bowl of Cheerios rather than Grape-Nuts for breakfast or ordering a latte over frappuccino, we are constantly making choices.

Making good choices requires constant focus and attention. Bad choices that seemed so right at the time sometimes turn out to be major impediments to our lives. Want proof? Just read the divorce statistics for your community, or as you drive to work, notice the businesses that have closed.

Our daily challenge is to live our character, action and investment choices so naturally that we make the best choices almost subconsciously. This requires patience, honest reflection, adaptation, and commitment.

THE PRIVILEGE OF CHOOSING

Making choices is a privilege that gives us freedom to mold our lives, a freedom we should never take for granted.

A graduate researcher, after a week of following an inmate's schedule from dawn to dusk each day at a state penitentiary, reported that the most difficult part of prison life was its lack of choices. "Inmates are denied choice over when life happens, from when to arise each day to when to shower, exercise, work, eat or retire," she said. "It was one of the most traumatic experiences of my life."

Isn't it interesting – in our free and democratic society, punishment comes in the form of reducing one's ability to make even the most basic choices in their everyday lives. Those inmates will confirm that life without choices is no way to live, and when we make a bad decision, our choices are reduced.

Life is filled with pressures that force us to make constant and immediate choices. Yet as the prison researcher found, a life without choices would not be much fun.

Think it's too late to embrace a new philosophy? Or maybe you're worried that you can't make the right choices. It is never too late!

According to psychologist Abraham Maslow, "The story of the human race is the story of men and women selling themselves short." **Don't sell yourself short. You can make better choices beginning today to achieve what you want in life tomorrow.**

Choose to read on, learn, make the right choices, and become the successful person you want to be.

Part One

The Character Choices ...

the foundation of success.

"Character is the foundation upon which one must build to win respect. Just as no worthy building can be erected on a weak foundation, so no lasting reputation worthy of respect can be built on a weak character."
– R.C. Samsel

The No-Victim Choice ...

Don't Let Your Past Eat Your Future

"Never be bullied into silence. Never allow yourself to be made a victim. Accept no one's definition of your life, but define yourself."
– Harvey S. Firestone

P oor Gary.

That's what they call him ... "Poor Gary." He labors all day in that tiny rear cubicle. His co-workers feel sorry for Gary because he always gets the worst territories, the poorest accounts and the most impossible schedules. Just when he thinks he's closed the deal that will put him over quota, the bottom drops out, and, at the end of the month, Gary's numbers fall short of the standard.

As the next month begins, Poor Gary's shoulders are more stooped, his head more bowed and his expression more defeated. His performance lags farther behind expectation and his sales calls are lackluster. Think Gary's results will improve this month? Not likely.

A victim is defined as: "a person to whom life happens." Without question, Poor Gary falls into the victim category. However, Gary's woes could be caused by his choice to be a victim. He complains about bad management, bad luck, being in a bad situation. Gary is a victim of all bad things that happen to him.

At the other end of the hall in the same organization is Colin Myers. Colin began work in the same small cubicle and worked the same territory Gary now occupies. The difference between Colin and Gary is that Gary chooses to be a victim, and Colin made the no-victim choice.

Whenever the unexpected, bad luck and bad situations occurred, Colin chose to dig deeper to make good things happen. When an order didn't come through, Colin spent time evaluating why he did not get the order and made adjustments that would help on his next call. In other words, Colin didn't wait for life to happen to him … he made choices to make things happen that would move him forward.

Gary was stuck in the ready-aim-aim-aim-complain-complain-complain syndrome, but Colin made the choice to load-fire-reload-fire when the going got tough.

Colin's performance resulted in several promotions, which moved him from the tiny rear cubicle where he had started into the manager's office. Colin had the ability to deal with whatever came his way … and good things kept coming his way.

Meanwhile, Gary was the perpetual victim of bad luck. Coincidence? Probably not.

RESPONDING TO THE UNEXPECTED

Many people choose to be a victim because something unexpected happens ... something completely out of their control. Others have an uncanny ability to successfully deal with the unexpected. **Positively dealing with the unexpected – looking for solutions, not excuses – is a conscious choice to avoid the victim mentality.**

If you know someone who is a master at dealing with the unexpected, take a closer look at that individual, because you've truly met a special person. Jim Lawton was like that. Whatever came his way, Jim could handle. His dad died while Jim was a freshman in college, and as tuition money dwindled, Jim found enough work to support himself and pay his tuition so he could continue working on his degree.

When the company he went to work for after graduation downsized, Jim networked his way into a new company and into a new job. Notice I didn't say "a better job." No, Jim found a job and mined each opportunity the job offered to move ahead. Whatever life has tossed his way, Jim hasn't allowed anything to keep him from being successful.

Jim's strength – and what counts most – is his choice to avoid feeling like a victim. Instead, he made up his mind to deal with the unexpected. Jim knew that there was no "grand conspiracy" preventing life from being easy for him. Jim knew that it was not what happened to him but his response to what happened that would make the difference. Today, Jim is successfully accomplishing his personal and professional goals.

Let me repeat Jim's lesson – it's not what happens to us but how we choose to respond to what happens that determines our next move … the next path, the next relationship, the next risk.

The unexpected is going to happen, and it is your choice how you deal with it. You can be a victim … or choose to realize that the unexpected may prevent you from achieving success unless you choose to proactively deal with it and continue moving forward.

Success is not an event … it is a process that will have peaks and valleys along the way.

Do we occasionally fall into the victim trap? Of course … occasionally feeling like a victim is natural, but remaining in the victim trap will prevent you from achieving success. So it is up to us to make the choice that we will not allow ourselves to be victims.

Is it always easy? Of course not … but it's a choice you make. You control your next move. Will you sit and sulk, or will you commit to continuing toward your ultimate goal?

MOVE FORWARD, NO MATTER WHAT

Once you choose to proactively deal with the unexpected, then it is time to take responsibility and move forward, no matter what.

Didn't accomplish your objectives for last month? You have two choices – either take responsibility and decide that you'll work twice as smart this month to make your goals, or you can wonder, "Why me?" and look around and find someone to blame.

Without fail, when you embrace this "why me" attitude or "victim mentality," it will paralyze your attitude and your enthusiasm while preventing you from doing what you need to do next. **When you become the "victim," you give up the right to create your future and allow yourself to be buffeted by what life brings.**

Or you can step up to the plate in the face of victim mentality and say, "Bring it on! I will not become a victim of things beyond my control!" It's your choice.

NOT EVERYTHING BAD THAT HAPPENS IS OUR DOING

David Cook, a popular sports psychologist for several professional golfers, says that in a round of golf, at least three things happen that are unfair or are not deserved. You may hit the ball 300 yards down the middle of the fairway, and it may land in a divot. You may hit a perfect approach shot to the green, and the wind gusts right as the ball is approaching, knocking the ball into the bunker. Or you may hit the perfect putt that goes off line because it hits a spike mark.

The choices available are to complain about being a victim of bad luck or another player's failure to fix a divot or spike mark … or accept that not all things that happen are our doing. We may not have caused the situation, but now we have to deal with the result.

In life, as in golf, not everything bad is our doing. But even when bad things happen that we do not deserve, the next move is ours … blame the situation, adopt the victim mentality or accept the unexpected, take responsibility and move forward.

All too often, people choose to be victims. This victimization may mean the difference between excellence and a mediocre career. It can also mean failure instead of success.

THE CHOICE TO SUCCEED

The good news is that we can make the choice to avoid becoming victims and get on the road to success. There are always alternatives … without limits … unless you set them.

The late Thomas J. Watson, the brilliant man who founded IBM, pushed his leadership personnel toward the resiliency of stumbling five times and getting up six. What he wouldn't tolerate was the paralysis of becoming a victim. "If you solve it wrong, it will come back and slap you in the face," Watson said. "Then you can solve it right. Lying dead in the water and doing nothing is comfortable because it is without risk, but it is an absolutely fatal way to manage."

In every situation, whether in your work life or your personal life, there are always alternatives – if you choose to see them. **If you choose to put on the blinders of victimization, prepare to accept that you will not reach your potential or achieve the success you deserve.**

As a wise man once counseled, "Don't let your past eat your future."

Three things you can do to make
the *no-victim* choice:

1 Expect the unexpected. Things beyond your control will happen. What you do control is how you respond to the unexpected things that come your way.

2 Look for alternatives. There are always alternatives if you choose to look for them. Don't paralyze yourself by falling into the victim trap.

3 Spend your energy searching for solutions, not excuses. No matter what happens, keep moving, one step in front of the other, toward your personal and professional goals.

"Things turn out best for the people who make the best of the way things turn out."
– John Wooden

The Commitment Choice ...

Passionate Enough to Succeed

"When work, commitment and pleasure all become one and you reach that deep well where passion lives, nothing is impossible."
– Anonymous

Most of us have been through this familiar drill: we set a goal – let's say it's to improve our fitness level. We set up a training program. Maybe we ask someone at the gym to give us some pointers.

Now comes the hard part – regular workouts. We'll do cardiovascular endurance training three times a week and weight training twice a week – one day for the upper body and one day for the lower body.

We set out with a calendar of our activities. The first day, we run two miles. Check. The second day, we lift weights. Check.

The third day ... well, we had to work late that day, so when we got home, it was too dark to run safely.

The fourth day … had a dinner appointment right after work. No weight training.

"Okay," we say to ourselves. "We've missed two days. We'll just begin again on Monday."

Monday comes, and, well, one of our co-workers is being promoted and transferred to another state, so we can't miss her going-away party.

Pretty soon, it's the end of the month, and we've checked off only two days of our training schedule. "Time flies," we mutter as we flip the calendar to the next month.

So what happened?

Apparently, our commitment to improving our fitness wasn't as important as we thought … or was it that something in our commitment was lacking?

COMMITMENT REQUIRES PASSION

Commitment isn't as simple as being able to check off what we've accomplished toward our goal. It's a choice … an attitude. It is believing that what you are doing is important enough to stay the course … it's about staying focused, about keeping your goal visible and successfully achieving that goal.

People who are successful have a passionate commitment to success and are willing to pay the price to achieve it.

Passionate? About commitment?

Absolutely!

Your dreams were the main motivator in the first place. You envisioned yourself fit, faster and less flabby than ever. You saw yourself crossing the finish line before most of the people years younger than yourself. You wanted the next promotion.

Often we enthusiastically set our goals, map our journeys and then make no forward progress. What happened to the enthusiasm we felt as we set our goals and made our plans?

Chances are, we weren't passionate about reaching those goals. We weren't committed enough to follow through to the end of the journey.

Benjamin Franklin made a list of traits he either wanted to get rid of or traits he wanted to cultivate, and then he graded himself on his progress or regression every day. Not yearly, weekly or monthly ... every day. His question to himself was "Did I get closer to accomplishing my goals today, or did I lose ground today?"

Franklin chose to be committed enough to his goals to take the time to measure his progress. He was committed enough to keep his goals in view ... working in some way each day to make one step forward. That's passionate commitment!

DEGREES OF COMMITMENT

By surrounding yourself with others who choose commitment and passion, you'll find yourself making more progress – since we tend to feed off those with similar goals and commitment levels.

Of course, there are degrees of commitment. But be aware that some are more committed than others, depending on their personal needs and goals.

Several years ago, the Great Gadzoni had just completed a challenging and dangerous tightrope walk over Niagara Falls. The wind was howling around the aerialist's ears, and stinging rain pelted him as he inched across the rope.

Met with enthusiastic applause from those waiting on the other side, the Great Gadzoni was wringing the water from his cape when an excited fan approached, urging him to make a return trip, this time pushing a wheelbarrow, which the fan just happened to have with him.

The Great Gadzoni was hesitant, having barely made the first trip across in the high winds and pouring rain. But the spectator insisted. "You can do it — I know you can," he urged.

The Great Gadzoni thought a moment. "You really believe I can do it?"

The spectator nodded excitedly, "Yes, yes. Definitely – you can do it."

"Okay," said the aerialist, taking the wheelbarrow from the man. "Get in."

Makes one wonder whether the spectator's passion for the feat lost its luster at the last minute when he was asked to commit, to invest in the goal.

But isn't this often where we find ourselves, just as we've sketched out the final details of a plan to reach a new goal?

The missing ingredient is the choice to commit ourselves, to go where no man or woman has gone before and, along the way, perhaps to endure what no one else would want to endure in order to discover success we have never known.

How Powerful Are You?

Do you find yourself in the place where you want to – but can't – make a commitment?

The reality is, **most people don't have a clue about how powerful they really are** – and they'll never find out until they choose to make a commitment to give what they consider to be "the impossible" a shot.

Some people report feeling overwhelmed when they try to reach new goals. Others describe the sensation as "being stuck." Still others say they reached for a goal once and were unsuccessful, so they've given themselves enthusiastic permission not to try again.

Don't allow fear of failure to cause you to fail.

Like the players on the successful CBS television series, Survivor, a commitment (to be the last person standing) often means doing what some people can't bring themselves to do (existing on bugs, slathering themselves in mud, etc.).

It's the same whether setting a personal or professional goal. Often you have to make the choice to commit – with passion – to do what others can't or won't do. The next step is investment – time, money, yourself, or whatever else is needed. Then be prepared to sacrifice.

What Is Passionate Commitment?

In 1982, the Ironman Triathlon was broadcast for the first time on NBC-TV. The bright sunshine of Hawaii's Kona Coast glittered on the backs of hundreds of athletes as they plunged into the ocean for the 2.5-mile swim. Once out of the water, they were on their way for a 100-mile bike ride around the island before completing the third leg, a 26.2-mile (marathon) run to the finish line. Any wonder why they call it Ironman?

Viewers who saw that race will never forget the images of 23-year-old Julie Moss crawling across the finish line in the darkness, totally dehydrated, her legs unable to support her for the final yards. This was her first Ironman competition, and her goal was to finish. She had dreamed of crossing the finish line, envisioned herself waving to the crowd as she broke the tape.

Few would have suffered the humiliation of a body so out of control it could barely crawl, but Moss was committed to finishing – and she did, dragging herself and crawling over the finish line only 29 seconds behind the first-place woman, Kathleen McCartney. Millions witnessed her feat and were inspired by her example.

Julie Moss was not just committed – she exhibited passionate commitment.

So what do people who choose passionate commitment do?

In most cases, they aren't as battle-fatigued as Julie Moss, but they often make great sacrifices to reach their goals. Here are a few of the attributes of people who have passionate commitment:

1. They do what they say they'll do – because **they committed to do it** ... and you can count on them ... every time. When they tell you they will do something, you can consider it done.

2. Like Julie Moss, they believe they can achieve a goal so strongly that **they envision themselves succeeding** in crossing the finish line. They can vividly see success.

3. They can verbalize their commitments. This doesn't mean sitting around talking about what they plan to do. **They put their goals into words** and then get busy.

4. **They're realistic.** They don't overpromise and underdeliver. Whatever they say, you can believe it.

5. People who choose commitment **invest in achieving their goals.** It may be the time in the classroom necessary to earn a college degree, energy on the basketball court practicing three-pointers, or hours at the computer, pounding out that first novel. When they commit, they invest.

6. Committed people **don't beat themselves up for falling short.** They use that experience to learn and continue the process.

7. People who choose to commit **plan their lives around what it takes to achieve a goal.** They are focused and make their success a top priority.

8. Most committed people **don't understand the term** *fail.* They think it means one step closer to success.

9. Like Julie Moss, people choosing to commit themselves to a

goal **impact the lives of those around them.** Enthusiasm and commitment are contagious.

Do you possess any of these attributes? Of course you do. We all have dreams and goals. We all want to move ahead or higher or farther down life's road.

The difference between those who achieve their goals and those who set them aside is the choice of commitment … being passionate enough to succeed.

Three things you can do to make
the **commitment** choice:

1 Stay the course. If your goal is worth committing to, it is worth the price that comes with passionate commitment.

2 Surround yourself with people who are equally committed – and passionate.

3 Clarify your commitment. Put your goals into words and then begin making your commitment a reality. Always be able to answer in fewer than twenty words – without hesitation – what you want to accomplish in the next two years.

*"The quality of a person's life is in direct proportion
to their commitment to excellence,
regardless of their chosen field of endeavor."*
– Vince Lombardi

The Values Choice ...

Choosing the Right Enemies

*"A wise man learns more from his enemies
than a fool from his friends."*
– Baltasar Gracian

Did you ever meet anyone who had no enemies?

Unfortunately, by the time most people have lived long enough to become adults, they've accumulated more than a few enemies, probably even more than they'd like to admit.

It is interesting to note that our civilization has used the word "enemy" since the 13th century, with meanings (according to the Merriam-Webster's Dictionary), including the following:

1. one that is **antagonistic** to another; especially: one seeking to injure, overthrow, or confound an opponent

2. something **harmful** or deadly

3. a military **adversary** or a hostile unit or force

No matter which definition you use, the more successful you become, the more enemies you're going to have.

THERE WILL BE ENEMIES FOR MANY REASONS

One Sunday morning while preaching on the theme "Love Thy Enemies," the late Dr. Martin Luther King Jr. told his congregation flatly, "The fact is, some people will not like you, not because of something you have done to them, but they just won't like you. Some people aren't going to like the way you walk; some people aren't going to like the way you talk. Some people aren't going to like you because you can do your job better than they can do theirs.

"Some people aren't going to like you because other people like you, and because you're popular, and because you're well-liked, they aren't going to like you. Some people aren't going to like you because your hair is a little shorter than theirs or your hair is a little longer and some are going to dislike you, not because of something that you've done to them, but because of various jealous reactions and other reactions that are so prevalent in human nature."

The question is not whether there will be enemies. You can't please everybody. You cannot invest your self-worth solely in what others think about you – you would never achieve success. You have to keep focused on your goals and objectives, and when the enemies come along, don't be surprised … welcome them. **Enemies are a by-product of success.**

The more successful you are in your career, the more susceptible you are to critics and a growing number of enemies, both inside and outside your office building.

As Abraham Lincoln expressed: "You can please all of the people some of the time and some of the people all the time, but you cannot please all the people all the time."

As we work to succeed, it is generally human nature to want to be accepted and respected – even loved – by our co-workers, management and customers. But the truth is, you can't please all the people all of the time, so at some point you have to choose whom you aren't going to please.

CHOOSING YOUR VALUES

A highly successful pediatrician had begun a private practice six years earlier. As the practice grew, his time at home became less and less. His wife – and the mother of his two children (both under the age of four) – had continued to urge him to get a partner to share emergency calls, but the conscientious physician declined, explaining that he felt a certain duty to his patients, and until he was sure another physician would take the same interest, he wasn't keen on the idea.

The physician's patients thought he was the best doctor they had ever had, but as the demands of the practice became heavier and his time at home had decreased to only a few hours on the weekend, the wife's urging became stronger. "I feel like a single parent, taking care of the kids day in and day out," she said during their most recent confrontation. "I need your time as much as some of your patients," she argued. "I need a life, too – so either find a partner or I'm finding another husband."

Faced with that choice, the physician eventually found another pediatrician who shared his values to join his practice. Some of the patients felt abandoned by the original practitioner when his new partner rotated weekend calls, but his home life definitely improved.

He had chosen his enemies – and he definitely didn't want the enemy to be his wife.

NO NEED TO CREATE ENEMIES … THEY WILL SURFACE ON THEIR OWN
In no way am I suggesting that your goal should be to create enemies. What I am encouraging you to do is understand that others may choose to be your enemies. They may be jealous of your success, or they may not like the fact that you do your job better than they do theirs – or it may be that their values don't match yours.

In many organizations, there may be a handful of individuals who seemingly thrive on controversy and seek out ways to create and inflame disputes. These are the enemies you will be forced to choose – those who are in conflict with your personal values.

People who disagree with you are not necessarily your enemies … unless their disagreement centers on the values you are trying to uphold.

Whatever the consequences, never sacrifice your values. But be aware that by making the choice not to sacrifice your values, you'll create enemies – people whose values, goals and objectives are different from yours.

So, ask the question: Who are my enemies? It's something to think about.

In any business, **the key to successfully dealing with your enemies is being able to identify who they are and understand why they have chosen to be your enemies.** If they are enemies because they are jealous or threatened by your success, there is nothing you can do about that. If they are your enemies because of something that you have done to them in the past, address the situation and allow them the choice of leaving your enemy camp.

But be aware – mistaking an enemy for an ally is the most foolish and costly mistake of all.

IT MATTERS WHOM WE HANG WITH

Any parent would attest that one of the most important decisions made by their children is the friends they choose. Bad choices made by teenagers can have a potentially devastating impact on their lives.

Our choice of whom we hang with at work is just as important as our teenagers' choice of friends.

How important is it to identify and choose our enemies, avoiding the corrupting influence of those who do not respect or hold our values?

Here's a story to illustrate the answer: Centuries ago, the slave Aesop penned a fable about a mouse who always lived on the land. By an unlucky chance, this mouse formed an intimate acquaintance with a frog that lived, for the most part, in the water.

One day, the frog was intent on mischief. He tied the foot of the mouse tightly to his own. Thus joined together, the frog led his friend the mouse to the meadow where they usually searched for food. Gradually, the frog led the mouse toward the pond in which he lived. Then, upon reaching the banks of the water, the frog suddenly jumped in, dragging the mouse with him.

Enjoying the water immensely, the frog swam croaking about as if he had done a good deed. The unhappy mouse soon sputtered and drowned, his poor dead body floating about on the surface.

A hawk observed the floating mouse from the sky and dived down and grabbed it with his talons, carrying it back to his nest. The frog, still fastened to the leg of the mouse, was also carried off a prisoner and was eaten by the hawk.

The moral: It is important to choose wisely those whom you associate with. The wrong person – the "enemy" – will lead you down the wrong path ... or into the wrong pond. Unfortunately, those of us not equipped to swim will inevitably drown.

VALUES – A DEFINING DIFFERENCE

What makes us different from our enemies – those enemies we choose?

In a word, the defining difference is our values, but you must learn – and learn quickly – who shares those values and who places little worth on doing the right thing.

Other "enemies" in business – and in life – worth choosing are:

1. Back-stabbers – those who betray a confidence or those who constantly discredit others.
2. Those with short tempers – these people are often catalysts for anger and discord at any moment.
3. Those who drink too much at business functions – and lose control of their words and actions.
4. Rebels against authority – they are on a collision course with failure.
5. People who rarely do what they say they are going to do.

Choose your enemies ... and your friends ... very carefully. A bad choice can be devastating to your career.

Three things you can do to make
the *values* choice:

1 Surround yourself with people of like values, and maintain your allegiance to those values.

2 Take the time to identify those who have chosen to be your enemies and make an effort to understand why. If they are your enemies because of something you have done in the past – address the situation. If they are your enemies because of their jealousy or value clash – move forward with caution, knowing they are your enemies.

3 Understand you cannot please all the people all the time – and accept that differences in values will automatically make some people your friends and others your enemies.

"You shall judge a man by his foes as well as by his friends."
– Joseph Conrad

The Integrity Choice ...

Doing the Right Thing

*"Integrity is telling myself the truth,
and honesty is telling the truth to other people."*
– Spencer Johnson

Whom do you trust?

Stop right now and make a list of five individuals you consider to be trustworthy. They may be family members, friends, business associates, or community leaders – they can be anyone as long as you trust them.

Now look at your list and ask yourself, "What characteristics do these people have in common?" One trait they likely share is that you perceive them to be people who are honest and have integrity.

Now, make a list of five people you don't trust. What traits do these individuals share? You probably think of them as being dishonest, or perhaps you question their integrity.

Honesty, integrity and trust are inextricably linked. If people perceive you to be a person of integrity, over time you will earn their trust. Someone once said, "People of integrity expect to be believed, and when they're not, they let time prove them right."

Many times, the loss of integrity has become the difference between failure and success, between sorrow and happiness. The integrity choice – doing the right thing regardless of who is watching – is one of the most important choices you will ever make, personally or professionally.

Since the collapse of several megacorporations and public figures, the word *integrity* has become a necessary descriptor for what is searched for in leaders and employees in any discipline – from medicine and research to banking, real estate, manufacturing, sales, and any other endeavor.

Think back over your past experiences. If you are like most, some of the greatest disappointments may have come from trusted people saying they were going to do something – or telling you they had done something, only to find that they didn't. Or they could have been people who liked to "put one over" on the team, the boss, even you, believing there are no holds barred … as long as they don't get caught.

Getting caught has nothing to do with integrity. Integrity is doing the right thing even if there is no chance that you would be caught doing the wrong thing.

Integrity is our foundation. Everything we do reflects our integrity, whether we are making personal decisions or decisions involving our organization.

A Large Dose of Integrity

In the fall of 1982, seven people on the west side of Chicago died mysteriously. Investigators found that each of the victims had ingested an extra-strength Tylenol capsule before they died – capsules that were found to be laced with cyanide.

News of these incidents traveled fast, causing a massive nationwide panic. A typical corporation's response might have been to minimize the issue and start looking for others to blame for the problem ... or to say it was a minor, isolated incident.

Officials at McNeil Consumer Products, a subsidiary of Johnson & Johnson – makers of Tylenol – made a tough choice, one that tested their integrity.

They acted quickly, immediately alerting consumers across the nation not to consume any type of Tylenol product. Then, along with halting production and any Tylenol advertising, Johnson & Johnson's top management recalled approximately 31 million bottles of Tylenol with a retail value of more than $100 million. You may recall seeing the news pictures of shelf after shelf of Tylenol products being swept into large plastic bags to be disposed of.

A few days later, Johnson & Johnson offered to exchange all Tylenol capsules that had already been purchased for new Tylenol tablets at a cost of several million dollars more to the corporation. Immediately thereafter, the company offered a $100,000 reward for the capture of the individual or individuals involved in the tampering case.

In addition, when the Johnson & Johnson team developed a tamper-proof cap, it gave the competitors the specifications of the cap so they could use it, too.

Without a doubt, Johnson & Johnson had put customer safety first before worrying about the company's profit and other financial concerns. They passed the integrity test. Their actions became the benchmark of corporate integrity – doing the right thing regardless of the consequences.

Through the company's actions, it became obvious to their customers that Johnson & Johnson only wanted to do the right thing once the link between Tylenol and the seven deaths in Chicago had been made. Through their actions, Johnson & Johnson's top management let the nation know that whatever the costs, they would choose integrity – a choice that ultimately served them well as they sought to re-establish the safety of and confidence in their products.

WHY THE INTEGRITY CHOICE IS IMPORTANT

Like every other choice we've discussed, being a person who chooses integrity will enrich lives, relationships and our success in every endeavor.

Dishonesty – the polar opposite of integrity – often carries a lasting aftertaste. In many arenas, dishonesty is the basis for both individual and corporate downfall. Rarely does the individual who operates without integrity find long-term success.

Integrity is also not something that can be practiced only part of the time ... or only with certain people.

Peter Scotese, chairman emeritus of New York's Fashion Institute of Technology, made it easy to understand integrity when he said, "Integrity is not a 90 percent thing, not a 95 percent thing – either you have it or you don't."

Scotese learned about integrity early in life. His father died the same year he was born, in 1920. When he was eight, his mother enrolled Peter in a school for orphaned boys, where he washed dishes, cleaned buildings and waited tables in return for his education.

After serving in World War II, earning the Bronze Star and two Purple Hearts, he began a career in textiles at Indian Head Mills of New York before moving to Springs Industries, Inc., in 1969, becoming the first nonfamily president of that corporation. During his tenure, sales tripled and earnings quadrupled.

In 1981, Scotese was the recipient of the Horatio Alger Foundation Award. He was recognized as an outstanding American who has demonstrated individual initiative and a commitment to excellence, exemplified by remarkable achievements accomplished through honesty, hard work, self-reliance and perseverance. In his acceptance speech, he attributed his success to the way integrity had empowered his life.

WHY SUCCESS RELIES ON INTEGRITY

In any successful team effort, we find ourselves relying on the integrity of our teammates. To be successful, we have to commit to certain efforts and then carry through on that commitment. We have to share a level of integrity that forbids cutting corners, letting things slip through the cracks or performing less than 100 percent of what we say we will do.

The same holds true for customers. When customers place orders, they rely on the integrity of their sales representatives and the integrity of companies to receive the quality they expect.

The late J.C. Penney, founder of the JCPenney stores, was known for his integrity, and in his book, *The Ninth Decade*, he tells of working at the village grocery as a boy and of reporting to his father about how the grocer would mix two grades of coffee and sell the mixture at the highest price. Young Penney thought this was a smart trick, but his father pointed out that the practice was dishonest, making his point so strongly that the boy quit his job. From that time on, Penney made honesty and integrity the foundation of his decisions throughout his lifetime.

How important is integrity? No quality reveals a person's true character more than integrity. It is the cornerstone of our personal and professional lives.

In many cases, it is easier to overpromise and underdeliver. In the business world, one of the favorite mottos of the last century was, "Success at all costs." However, visionary business leaders were quick to learn that practices lacking integrity soon lose business as well as the respect of customers and colleagues.

No, it is not success at all costs – particularly if the cost of doing business is a compromise of personal or corporate integrity.

Succeed with Integrity

What are the characteristics of people with integrity – people who can be trusted when they give their word about anything, from keeping appointments to maintaining their loyalties?

1. They establish integrity as a top priority. It is the cornerstone of their actions and decisions.

2. They have clear, uncompromised values and communicate them without hesitation.

3. They do what is right and ethical regardless of the circumstances – no hidden agendas, no political games, and no regrets.

4. They never compromise their integrity by rationalizing a situation as "an isolated incident." There are no "isolated incidents." They have decided where their integrity boundaries exist and stay within them.

5. They never allow achieving results to become more important than the means to their achievement. How they win is just as important as winning.

6. They do what they say they will do. Their integrity is judged every time they say they are going to do something – regardless of how insignificant they consider the commitment.

The choice of integrity is one of the most important choices you can make because integrity not only guides our every action but also chooses the paths necessary for long-term success.

Whether you're talking about individuals or organizations – where there is no integrity, there is no trust. Trust is a by-product of integrity. **Somewhere along the way, as you seek wealth, knowledge, success or votes, integrity – your integrity – will be put to the test.**

There is never a good reason to sacrifice your integrity! People will forgive and forget judgment errors ... they never forget integrity mistakes.

Choose to do the right thing, even if it hurts. Guard your integrity as though it is your most precious personal possession ... because that is exactly what it is.

Three things you can do to make
the *integrity* choice:

1. Guard your integrity as though it is your most important possession ... because that is exactly what it is.

2. Realize that there are no "time outs" with your integrity. It is also not something that can be practiced only part of the time ... or only with certain people ... protecting your integrity is an all-the-time deal.

3. Do the right thing. It isn't always easy – in fact it is sometimes really hard – but just remember that doing the right thing is always right.

"*A good name is more desirable than great riches; to be esteemed is better than silver or gold.*"
Proverbs 22:1 (NIV)

PART TWO

The Action Choices ...
the movement toward success.

"A man is the sum of his actions, of what he has done, of what he can do. Nothing else."
– Mahatma Gandhi

The Do-Something Choice ...

Don't Vacation
on Someday Isle

"Have you ever said: 'I'll be happy when ... I lose 20 pounds, live in a bigger house ... get a new boyfriend/girlfriend ... make more money, etc.?' You get the picture. Someday Isle is not a dream vacation spot.
It is an imaginary destination to which you will never arrive.
It is the carrot on the stick perpetually in front of you.
So close you can see it, yet you will never reach it.

Don't vacation on Someday Isle."

– Frank F. Lunn, author of *Stack the Logs!*

Quick! Answer this riddle: Three frogs are sitting on a lily pad. One decides to jump off. How many frogs remain on the lily pad?

If you said three, you're right. Deciding to jump off and actually doing it are two completely different things.

A day seldom passes without someone telling me that he or she wants to write a book. The person has a good idea and the desire to make a difference in others' lives. My advice is always the same ... great, people would love to hear your story ... get on with it.

Writing a book takes time, commitment and passion – done mainly in solitude. Like 20th-century American writer William Faulkner found, it also takes persuasive persistence to get the words on paper.

Most of the time, the book remains an intention and never gets written. Seldom is a chapter written, and most of the time not a word is written on paper. That person may have a great book inside his or her head and may have decided to write a book … but the book will not write itself. Such people are vacationing on Someday Isle! The only way to get off Someday Isle is to get going and do something.

How many times this week have you decided to do something and then didn't follow through? For many people, this is a routine choice – but how often have they looked back, regretting that they didn't pursue a goal … or take the time to explore a new idea … because they were waiting for some better day or time.

To achieve success, you have to make the choice to **do something.**

Never be content with the status quo. The status quo may be comfortable, but **you cannot improve while you are in the rut of doing the same things over and over.** Someone once said the only difference between a rut and a grave is the depth. You have to do something to avoid living your life in a rut.

THE DONKEY AND THE WELL

One day a donkey fell into a well. When the owner discovered what had happened, he frantically searched for ways to rescue the animal, with no success. Regretfully, the owner decided that since the donkey was growing old, he should give up the idea of rescuing the animal and simply fill in the well. Hopefully, the donkey's demise would be quick and painless.

The farmer then called his neighbors to help with the task, and soon several men began shoveling dirt into the well.

When the donkey realized what was happening, he brayed and struggled … but finally the noise stopped.

After a few sad moments, the farmer looked into the well and there stood the donkey. Alive and progressing to the top, the donkey had found that by shaking off the dirt instead of allowing it to bury him, he could keep stepping on top of the earth as its level rose. Then, he could easily step out of the well – and trot off happily.

As you may have noticed, life often attempts to cover us over with dirt and clutter. The trick is to shake it off and do something to take the next step up.

DO SOMETHING TO CHANGE YOUR LIFE – READ EVERY DAY

Charlie "Tremendous" Jones, my friend and wise counsel, says "You are today what you'll be five years from now, except for the people you meet and the books you read." Think about that. In five years, you can be completely different or just like you are right now – it is your choice.

Do you think it is coincidental that, in most cases, the bigger the house, the bigger the library inside the house? Career success requires that you are continuing to increase your knowledge. Many top executives of organizations will read up to ten books a month, yet average American workers will probably not read ten books in their lifetimes.

There is a direct correlation between the books you read and the success you achieve.

The next time you visit someone's home, check out the books on the table next to his or her favorite chair. See what kind of books are on their bookshelves. You can tell what has molded the philosophy and values of a person by the books he or she reads.

The good news is that there is an abundance of books available to teach you or inform you about any subject you are interested in.

Would you like to sit down and talk to Albert Einstein? Then read one of his essays. What would you like to ask Churchill about his life experiences? Pick up any of hundreds of books and read how he would answer your question. Would you enjoy hearing Ronald Reagan tell how it felt to tell Gorbachev "Tear these walls down!"? Read his memoirs. How about listening to Peter Drucker talk about management and leadership? Read his books. Or if you want to become a more complete thinker, read the Bible, as the vast majority of great thinkers have done, whether they believed it or not.

You may be limited in the people you will meet in your lifetime. Many of the people we would like to meet and enjoy learning from are not alive or may not be available to us. But you are not limited in what you can learn from others. Reward yourself with the knowledge of great people and become a better person because of the information waiting for you in books.

Don't stifle your career by limiting your knowledge.

Where do you start? Anywhere. Just start enjoying the company of the greats or the pleasantness of the interesting by reading!

I suggest to people who ask that they should read Fred Smith's *You and Your Network*. The wisdom contained in that book is timeless and can be the launching pad for you to get the most out of your life and your career. Start with that book or start somewhere else. Just get started!

Mark Layton, a successful businessman and one of my mentors, has hired hundreds of recent college graduates over the years. After studying and evaluating the difference between the successful ones and the ones who did not make it in business, he discovered one common denominator among those who fail: they think that their learning is complete when they get the diplomas. They quit investing in learning. The long-term successful graduates were those who had the discipline to continue to spend hours daily, even in their later career years, learning and improving.

The more you learn, the more you will be able to earn. It is your choice. Don't go through a day without reading – it will change your life.

THE BEST KEEP DOING SOMETHING TO BECOME EVEN BETTER

As the old saying goes, people can be divided into three categories – those who make something happen, those who watch things happen and those who wonder what happened. Successful people make things happen by taking action and not allowing themselves to be swept along by what life brings.

There are plenty of great examples of how the "do-something" choice works. Take a look at some of the many athletes who made the choice to do something, even though they were already the best in the world.

Olympian Carl Lewis, even after setting world records in track and field, made the choice to continue working and training with his college coach so he could run a little faster and jump farther than his last record.

After dominating the junior tournaments, long after other golfers had gone into the clubhouse, young Tiger Woods remained on the course, practicing his shots. He was not content just to win. He chose instead to do whatever it took to be the best ever to play the game of golf.

Most successful people are never satisfied with their last score, their last record or their last performance. How many great authors have written just one book? How many great leaders have quit after one successful year? How many great coaches have quit after their first win?

WINNERS KEEP WINNING

While working for Xerox early in my career, one of my yearly goals was to win the annual President's Club award. Each year the top performers would be recognized with a great trip. After enjoying a couple of those President's Club trips, one observation that was obvious to me was that 80 percent (my estimate) of the winners were the same people every year.

Were all those repeat winners just the lucky salespeople with the best territories? Of course not. Many changed territories multiple times but still made the President's Club trip. These successful people made the choice to keep getting better, even though they were already at the top of their fields.

In the years since that observation, I have confirmed in every business that I have been associated with that the winners keep winning. A tough year may come along occasionally, but over the long haul, **the winners keep winning because they keep doing the necessary "somethings" to win.**

Rarely is anything gained by soaking up the limelight of that last success. Do something!

DO SOMETHING TO CLEARLY COMMUNICATE

Regardless of the career you choose, to be successful in that career, you have to be able to get your point across.

Fair or not, people tend to typecast you by how well you speak, write and listen. Every word spoken, every sentence written, and how well you listen sends a message of your commitment to success.

More than any other single attribute, the use of a vast vocabulary is an immediate indication of your intelligence. Ironically, most people's vocabularies stagnate before the age of 30. It is a fact that your chances for success will increase in proportion to the strength of your vocabulary and how well you communicate.

Speaking to groups – of two or three or even a roomful – is required for advancement in almost every industry. Opinions are formed based on how well you deliver a message. The message may be as simple as "say a few words about yourself" or as important as "tell us why your team needs a budget increase." Successful people spend time, energy and focus on improving their verbal communication skills.

Another communication skill required for success is the ability to write clearly and concisely. Even when you are not present, you are represented by what and how you write. Those who receive your memos, e-mails, reports and other documents automatically form an impression of you.

The third communication skill required for success is the ability to listen effectively. Studies have shown that miscommunication occurs largely because people do not take the time to listen.

What can you do to improve your communication skills? There are plenty of choices available: communication classes are available on line or at your local college, public speaking groups are easily found, writing courses are abundant and, of course, there are books on every communication subject. Choose whatever fits your schedule. Just do something to become an effective communicator.

DOING SOMETHING TAKES COURAGE

Think you've reached the top of your game? Don't see a reason to keep improving? Make the choice to challenge yourself. Don't let your current success lull you into the delusion of contentment.

The difference between those who succeed and those who allow fear to immobilize them is the choice to courageously keep moving forward when things get tough.

Throughout literature, the theme of "courage" is second only to the theme of "love." Most of us would readily admit that courage is the one virtue we want for ourselves. "If I had one wish," wrote a Harvard scholar, "it would be never to be scared and never to feel the shame of being scared."

Sure, everybody has fears. From the part-time employee at the local car wash to the moguls who shape and guide corporations, we all fear the unknown. We're all afraid of failure … and the list of fears goes on and on.

When you make the choice to do something, to keep moving, your fear will diminish, your confidence will increase, and in the process you remove the unknown. Attack what you fear, and the fear will eventually disappear.

One of the greatest mistakes you can make is to be paralyzed by the fear that you will make a mistake. **The key to overcoming fear is to continue moving forward, despite your fears.**

Historically, the survivors of any great challenge are those who kept moving forward. From the men and women of the ill-fated wagon train who found their way through the blizzards of Donner Pass to modern-day hiker Aron Ralston, who chose to keep moving by amputating his arm with a pocketknife after being pinned under an 800-pound boulder for five days, doing nothing would have been fatal. "Dying wasn't an alternative," Ralston said, after freeing himself and walking five miles before being found by two hikers who helped him to safety.

Doing nothing can be fatal to your success. Make the same choice as Aron Ralston and keep moving forward despite your fear.

GET PAST SPLAT

But there are some who give up too soon … just before they turn the corner to success. **Successful people keep moving even when they are scared and have made mistakes … unsuccessful people quit before they have a chance to be successful.**

The following story illustrates what happens to many on the road to success. A man meets a guru in the road. The man asks the guru, "Which way is success?"

The bearded sage doesn't speak, but points to a place in the distance.

The man, thrilled by the prospect of quick and easy success, rushes off. Suddenly, there comes a loud "splat." Eventually, the man, now tattered and stunned, limps back, assuming he must have taken a wrong turn, so he repeats his question to the guru, who again points silently in the same direction.

The man obediently walks off, and this time the splat sound is deafening. When the man crawls back, he is bloody, broken and irate. "I asked you which way to success," he screams at the guru. "I followed your direction, and all I got was splatted! No more of this pointing! Talk!"

Only then does the guru speak, and what he says is this: "Success is that way. Just a little past splat."

How many of us are strong enough to make the effort long enough to get past splat?

Do Something to Look Successful

One "do something" choice everyone can make is to look successful. If you want to be successful, one of the first things you have to do is look successful.

The two things that immediately influence other people are the expression on your face and the clothes you wear. Even if you don't think you have the money to spend on expensive clothes, buy the best you can afford. Your clothes are an investment in your success.

In competitive situations, the candidate who looks healthy, happy and energetic always has a better chance of being promoted. You don't have to be an Adonis to win a promotion, but it is definitely to your advantage to take care of each aspect of your life – physical, emotional, spiritual and intellectual – and a dab of shoe polish and ironing that shirt you plan to wear tomorrow helps, too.

Take a look around. The people you admire and respect on the job or in your family are usually those who look and act like people worthy of admiration and respect.

Choose to do something to look successful. If you feel unattractive, have a makeover. If you want to wear a smaller size, exercise – and lose the weight. If you want to feel more energized, take a brisk walk every morning before work. It's amazing how those endorphins you create with exercise will make you feel. Choose to do something – for yourself.

Do Something Different Now

Finally, choose to do something that will make a difference. If you aren't happy with the way things are now, choose to do something about it.

Want a better tomorrow? Do something different today. The things that are on your mind today will ultimately be in your future. What you are thinking about, you will ultimately do.

Changing your life could be as simple as changing your mind – if you make the choice to do something. Not happy? If you have time to whine and complain about something, you have time to do something about it.

One of the most important decisions you can make is to study what successful people do. Pay attention. What are the common "do something" choices of the people who represent success to you? The choices they make are probably the same choices that you can make to get closer to success.

Don't vacation on Someday Isle … do something to earn your success – beginning today!

Three things you can do to make
the **do-something** *choice:*

1 Spend more time on action and less time on thinking about what you want to do. Those who take action usually fare much better than those swept along by what life brings.

2 Study successful people. What choices have they made to improve help them reach their level of success?

3 Keep learning. Read every day. The difference between the successful and the mediocre is that the successful never stop learning.

"One of the marks of successful people
is that they are action-oriented.
One of the marks of average people
is that they are talk-oriented."
– Brian Tracy

The Persistence Choice ...

Learning from Failure

*"Many of life's failures are people who did not realize
how close they were to success when they gave up."*
– Thomas Edison

Amemorable speech by a successful businessman was introduced by a wise master of ceremonies who announced, "Our man of the hour spent many days and nights getting there."

There is no such thing as instant success. Success is not an overnight accomplishment ... it is the reward for persistence, sticking to it and learning from failure.

As early as the 6th century B.C., ancient Greeks identified certain traits that allowed common people to rise above the crowd. One of those traits – a characteristic vital to great long-term accomplishment – is persistence.

The slave Aesop described persistence in his ancient fable about a race between a slow tortoise and a swift hare. Halfway through the race, the hare is so far ahead and so confident of victory that he takes a nap. The tortoise, not nearly as swift, continues plodding along, eventually passing the hare, who awakens just in time to see his slow-moving opponent crossing the finish line.

Clearly the hare was faster and more athletic and should have won the race handily. His lack of persistence caused him to lose.

How often have we seen others with huge talents and great abilities end up going nowhere while many average men and women achieve greatness? Most of the time, the difference is their choice to persist … to stick to it long enough to win.

The choice of persistence is about setting a goal and reaching it, about coming to roadblocks and hurdling them, about continuing the journey in spite of life's speed bumps. Most of the time, success will be achieved by those who want it the most and will persevere past their failures.

Pass Go, Collect $200

Charles Parker loved playing games and included obstacles in many of the games he made up. While only a teenager, he invented his first game – called "Banking" – and at age 16 in 1883, decided to publish it.

Turned down by two publishers, Parker was undaunted. When many would have given up and pursued other endeavors, he borrowed and saved until he had $40 to print 500 sets of Banking. By the end of the year, he had sold all but 24 of the games, netting $100.

With his profits, he started the George S. Parker Company, and, after convincing his brothers, Charles and Edward, to join him, Parker Brothers was born. By 1890, the company had 29 games on the market, and when they introduced Monopoly in 1935, Parker Brothers had solidified its place as the game giant all over the world.

Like the required strategy to win in many of his games, Parker set an example that has taught us that you succeed only if you are persistent enough to stick to it long enough to win. Fortunately for almost all of us, Parker viewed his early failure as a healthy and inevitable part of the process on his way to success.

FAILURE IS, INDEED, AN OPTION.

After overcoming obstacles all of his life, Dr. Martin Luther King, Jr., also was convinced that "the measure of a man is not where he stands in moments of convenience, but where he stands in times of challenge and adversity."

In our society, *fail* has become an objectionable four-letter word, both personally and in business. We rarely use it, and many of us try not to think about it.

Young children learn early on that failing isn't acceptable behavior. In some cases, children are so frightened of failure that they often don't try new sports or accept new challenges because they have been conditioned to see failure as too harmful, too destructive to survive.

In a recent sales meeting, clips from the popular movie *Apollo 13* were shown before the CEO of the company spoke to the sales force. Borrowing a phrase from the movie, the CEO tried to motivate his colleagues toward a record-breaking year by saying, "Failure is not an option."

Isn't it interesting, though, that success is usually preceded by failure?

In fact, most successful people today are the result of persisting beyond failures, and usually not one, but many failures enable them to discover their route to success.

STICKING TO FAILURE

In 1968, 3M scientist Dr. Spencer Silver developed a new kind of glue, an unusual adhesive that formed tiny balls with the diameter of a paper fiber. These tiny spheres could not be melted and would not dissolve, but because these little balls made only intermittent contact, they didn't stick strongly. After several attempts to strengthen the adhesive, Dr. Silver set his glue aside as a useless failure.

Fast-forward to 1974, when fellow scientist Art Fry became frustrated one Sunday morning when his paper bookmark kept falling out of his hymnal as he sang in his church choir. Remembering Silver's failed adhesive, Fry went back to the lab, where he began working with the forgotten glue.

By coating the edge of a paper bookmark with this "failed" glue, Fry found that the coated paper would stay in place when needed, yet could be easily removed afterwards without otherwise harming the page it was attached to.

It took another four years to convince higher-ups his new product was valuable, and when a group of secretaries was called in to experiment with Fry's find, 3M found a multitude of uses for what the secretaries called "sticky notes" and soon began marketing them on a national scale.

By 1990, 3M's Post-It Notes were one of the five top-selling office-supply products in America.

Like these now-familiar sticky slips of paper, most revolutionary products are built on failed prototypes that sent inventors back to the drawing board to make changes.

LEARNING FROM FAILURE

Henry Ford made many return trips to the drawing board as he developed his first automobiles and then began work on creating the first assembly line. "Failure is only an opportunity to more intelligently begin again," he assured the skeptics of his time.

The same is true for most technology. After a failure, designers review their objectives, make changes to overcome the obstacles they encountered with the last model, and eventually arrive at a successful conclusion. Inventor Thomas Edison knew this route well. "Some of the best lessons we ever learn we learn from our mistakes and failures," he said.

Successful people learn from failure. In fact, **most successful people fail faster and more often than the average person ... their success is not an accident. They learn enough from failure to be successful.**

SUCCESS ... THE TOUGHER CHOICE.

Without a doubt, it is always the easier choice to be satisfied with failure and give up. Aircraft designer Burt Rutan has had more than his share of failures, but these unsuccessful experiences did not cloud his vision. Instead, he and his team of pilots and engineers continued reaching for their dreams of building, testing and flying the first commercially viable manned spacecraft.

In October 2004, when the sleek *SpaceShipOne* poked through the cloudless horizon of the Mojave Desert, reaching an altitude of 368,000 feet above the earth, Rutan and his team not only made way for commercial space flight, but they also won the coveted $10 million Ansari X Prize.

Awarded to the first privately funded commercial spacecraft successfully completing two trips of at least 62.5 miles into space and returning safely to Earth before January 2005, the Ansari X Prize was an incentive for jump-starting commercial space flight.

Obviously, it would have been much more comfortable for Rutan and his team to sidestep the risks required to continue after several hits – and misses. However, to win, you have to stay in the game. The rewards far outweigh the pain of past failures for those who choose to overcome obstacles.

When failure comes, don't hang your head ... hold your head high so you can look failure squarely in the eye and say, "I am bigger than you. You cannot make me quit. I am going to learn from you and whip you."

Stick to it and turn failure into success!

Three things you can do to make
the *persistence* choice:

1 When you reach roadblocks to your success, don't give up. Rarely does anyone succeed without overcoming obstacles.

2 Failure is a learning tool. Keep your eyes open to the opportunities that failure provides.

3 If you want to win, you have to stay in the game. Don't let temporary failure cause you to miss out on permanent success.

"Nothing in the world can take the place of persistence."
- Calvin Coolidge

The Attitude Choice ...
The Enthusiastic Approach

"There's very little difference in people. But that little difference makes a big difference. The little difference is attitude. The BIG DIFFERENCE is whether it is positive or negative."
- W. Clement Stone

A salesman moved into a new town and met an old-timer as he was leaving the bank. "I'm new to your town. What are the people like here?" the salesman asked.

"What were the people like in the town you came from?" the old-timer responded.

"Well, they were glum and negative and always complaining, and their glasses were always half-empty," the salesman replied.

"Hmmm," said the old-timer. "Sounds about like the people who live here."

A few weeks later, another person moved to the same town and met the same old-timer as he was leaving the same bank. "I'm new to your town. What are the people like here?" the newcomer asked.

"What were the people like in the town you came from?" the old-timer responded.

"Well, they were wonderful. They worked together in the neighborhood, helped each other out, and were always there to support us during tough times. We're going to miss them," the newcomer replied.

"Hmmm," said the old-timer. "I think you will like it here. That sounds about like the people who live here."

The old-timer's message? If you want to be around people who are positive and enthusiastic and eager to live life, your attitude has to be the same. If you think the people around you are glum and negative, you probably ought to check your attitude – because it's probably glum and negative, too.

If you want to be around happier people, choose to be happy yourself. It all starts with you and your choice. As an old farmer used to tell his children, "You can't change the fruit without changing the root." Our root is our attitude, and our fruit is how others see us.

The longer we live and the older we get, the more evidence we see that our attitude impacts every aspect of our lives. If you look closely, you'll find that attitude becomes the linchpin for your opportunities, your circumstances, your successes and your failures.

IS ATTITUDE AN AUTOMATIC RESPONSE?

Many people subscribe to the theory that attitudes are simply automatic responses to circumstances, that your attitude is simply a reflection of external circumstances. The automatic response to something negative is negative … and the automatic response to something positive is positive. Whatever happens to us dictates the way we respond.

I do not buy in to that theory.

Your attitude is completely INTERNALLY controlled … a personal response to conditions and circumstances … no one can externally control your own attitude.

Of course, all things that happen to us are not all within our control, but we do control how we respond to those events. We choose how we react … no one can make that choice for us.

We do not live in a Pollyanna world where only good things happen to good people. Far from it … everyone has things happen that are unexpected and unpleasant, and we have to deal with those events.

THE POWER OF OUR ATTITUDES

We may not want to admit this responsibility, but the facts are clear: We are in charge of our attitudes – and our happiness. The choices about the attitude we'll embrace are choices we make every day and a choice we make many times a day.

Your attitude is powerful.

When facing serious illnesses, doctors will confirm that many times the difference between survivors and those who do not survive is the attitude of the patient. In sports, coaches will confirm that the attitude of the team is a major portion of the game plan. In school, teachers will confirm that positive kids produce positive results. In business, a Gallup poll revealed that 90 percent of people say they are more productive when they are around positive people.

If positive attitudes make us happier, more productive and more successful ... why would anyone in the world choose negativism – a self-inflicted wound – and all the ramifications that come along with that choice? Why would people choose to hurt themselves by being negative?

Maybe they choose to be negative because they don't realize they have the power to be positive ... or perhaps they enjoy feeling sorry for themselves ... or it is more difficult to be positive.

I think it is because negative attitudes are a natural response ... and some people enjoy it! They say they are being "realistic," which in most cases means exposing the negative and cynical response to a situation ... refusing to even acknowledge the "just as realistic" positive response.

Successful people choose not to inflict the poison of negative attitudes on themselves.

Most people love to be around people who are positive and enthusiastic, always looking for the best. They attract others like a magnet ... they are the force multiplier. Positive and enthusiastic people add energy to those around them ... negative and cynical people zap the energy from those around them.

Answer this question: When was the last time you knew a successful person who people consistently described as negative and cynical?

In my years of experience, I cannot name one successful person described that way. Not one.

Coincidental? I don't think so. Optimism and enthusiasm are two traits that you will find in most top employees and leaders, regardless of industry, profession or age.

CULTIVATING ENTHUSIASM

Successful people cultivate the habit of enthusiasm in the same way as others cultivate the habit of waking early or exercising. It takes time, perseverance, planning and commitment.

The power of enthusiasm is evidenced by the effect it has on other people. We have all witnessed the enthusiastic school kid selling candy door to door. They are enthusiastic because they are confident in themselves, love their product and enjoy achieving a goal. We are happy to buy from them.

We have also witnessed kids who are just trying to sell candy because that is what they have to do. There is no passion, enthusiasm or energy. The candy is the same, the customer is the same, yet the sales are not even close. The missing ingredient is enthusiasm.

Real enthusiasm and a positive attitude are not things you put on or take off to fit the occasion or to impress people. **Real enthusiasm is a way of life, yet many people allow conditions to control their attitude rather than allowing their attitude to help control conditions.**

A positive attitude is more important to our success than how we dress, how we look, how much skill we have, how much education we've accumulated, and how gifted we think we are.

ENJOYING THE OPPORTUNITY TO SUCCEED

The good news is that we have an opportunity to choose the attitude we will have for each situation every day, whether it is a change in job assignments, the way we spend our lunch hour, or our attitude while we're in the car, driving to work each day.

Truitt Brinson began his career in insurance sales by repeating, "Today is my day of opportunity" every day before going to his office. He repeated it so often that his children were soon chanting the same daily mantra – and grew to use it in their own lives.

Several years later, he recalled the practice as he accepted Mutual of New York's coveted Man of the Year Award. "It's all about attitude," he said, "and my attitude is that I enjoy the opportunities to succeed every day."

All too often we may want to blame our attitude about something on past events and experiences in our lives.

Author Charles Dickens once advised, "Reflect upon your present blessings, of which every man has many – not on your past misfortunes, of which all men have some."

Don't brood over mistakes, carry grudges or harbor hate – each of those negative emotions possesses the power to prevent you from accomplishing the success you desire.

EXPECT CHALLENGES

It is easy to have a positive attitude when things are going well. But, unfortunately life is full of times when things do not work the way we plan. When challenges emerge in your path, the best antidote is to focus on what you desire, not what you fear. Allow your attitude to work for you by visualizing, believing, and taking action. Visualize future successes, believe you will achieve them, and then move forward toward your goal.

When you invest yourself in working toward a goal, there is no time to think about the hurdles. Just keep moving.

Do you think your past has created a "natural negative attitude"? Unfortunately, we cannot change our past ... or the fact that people act in a certain way. Remember, your attitude is not externally controlled ... it is INTERNALLY controlled. If we have a negative attitude, it's because we've made the choice to have that negative attitude right now.

Bottom line, success is not dependent upon what happens to us ... success is dependent upon how we react to what happens.

OPPORTUNITY OR CALAMITY

Winston Churchill once said, "An optimist sees an opportunity in every calamity, a pessimist sees a calamity in every opportunity."

There is an enduring story that illustrates Churchill's point. Two researchers working for a large shoe manufacturer were independently dispatched to one of the world's least-developed countries. Their task was to evaluate the business potential within that country.

After several weeks, the first report came back to the manufacturer's headquarters, and the message read, "No market here. Nobody wears shoes." A few days later, the second report came back from the other researcher. It read, "Great market here. Nobody wears shoes!"

Optimists see opportunity. Pessimists are blind to opportunity.

Fortunately, **optimism can be learned and developed … it is your choice.** You can choose how you react to events and challenges and become the architect of your own happiness.

There are basic differences in the choices made by optimistic and pessimistic people:

An Optimist vs. a Pessimist	
An optimist looks for potential opportunities within difficulties.	A pessimist sees only problems and makes difficulties of opportunities.
An optimist sees setbacks as temporary and minor.	A pessimist chooses to see setbacks as permanent and catastrophic.
An optimist chooses to energize others and find creative solutions.	A pessimist zaps energy and destroys your confidence.
An optimist feels he or she has sufficient control to make things happen.	A pessimist feels that everybody but him or her is in control.
An optimist sees the doughnut.	A pessimist sees the hole.

EYES-WIDE-OPEN ATTITUDE

About a century ago, among Atlanta pharmacist John Pemberton's inventions were hair dye, cough syrup and liver pills. He had been working on a new invention – a headache syrup – but just couldn't seem to get it right.

One day he went to a back room of his pharmacy to discover two of his young employees mixing his new headache syrup with water and drinking it because, as they explained, they liked the taste.

As opposed to being angry at his workers for loafing on the job, Pemberton chose to be curious about their claim and tried the remedy himself. "Not bad," he thought as he added a little club soda to give the drink some fizz. "Even better," he pronounced.

Pemberton saw potential in a situation that would have been frustrating or even infuriating to most of us.

Soon after, the pharmacist began selling his new-found drink in his pharmacy, calling it "Coca Cola"… and the rest, as they say, is history.

GROWING OPTIMISM

Want to be a more optimistic person?

You can find the path in the **Six Laws of the Growing Optimism:**

1. **You Reap Only What You Sow** – If you've sown apple seeds, you'll get apples. Don't expect oaks from apple seeds. If you want to be more optimistic, sow seeds of optimism. Sow positive behaviors to reap positive results – and surround yourself with positive people.

2. **You Need to Know Where to Sow** – Seeds sown on rocks will never bear fruit. Find fertile ground and sow your seeds there. Commit to positive projects, people and tasks. Spend your energies to achieve positive goals, never wasting precious resources.

3. **At Some Point, You Must Reap Your Harvest** – One farmer loved to cultivate and till the soil into neat rows and then sow his seed, but when it came time for harvest, he hated to drive the combine into the fields, crushing the neat mounds

of soil and leaving nothing but chaff in its wake. If we sow – if we make the effort, then we must reap. Otherwise, why bother?

4. **We Can't Do Anything About Last Year's Harvest** – Life is filled with important choices, and every choice has a consequence. It's not about whether last year's harvest was good or bad. It's about how we handled the success or failure of that harvest. Did our failure prevent us from sowing positive seeds today? We can do something about only this year's crop ... but we can also take what we learned last year and make this year's harvest more bountiful.

5. **Don't Worry About the Weather, the Beetles, – or Anything Else** – Worrying is a wasted effort and the breeding ground of doubt. It will lead you to focus on potential losses rather than effective solutions. Your best choice to stop worry is positive action.

6. **Be Easy on Yourself** – It's important to have the strength and the desire to continue sowing. Beating yourself up for a poor harvest only wastes time. You can never like anyone else more than you like yourself – and don't expect others to like you if you don't hold yourself in high esteem.

THE LIFE-SAVING VALUE OF OPTIMISM

Max was always optimistic and a natural motivator, one of the principal reasons why he was successful in retail. Every day was a good day for business. His clerks liked what they saw in Max and emulated his approach to life. He was not only their hero, but also successful in his career.

Early one morning, a robber made his way into Max's office, demanding the manager to lie down on the floor and to give him the combination to the safe. After taking the money, the thief shot Max so he couldn't identify his assailant.

Luckily Max was found soon afterward and was rushed to the hospital. After he had recovered, Max was asked whether he was afraid at any time in the aftermath of the shooting.

"Everyone was great," Max recalled. "But when I arrived in the emergency room, I could see that the doctors and nurses thought I was a goner … which is when I made the biggest choice of my life.

"A big, burly nurse was shouting questions at me," Max remembered. "Then she asked whether I was allergic to anything. 'Yes,' I replied, and the medical team stopped working, waiting for more information. So I took a deep breath and yelled, 'Bullets!' Then, while they were still laughing, I added, 'And I am choosing to live, so see what you can do.'"

Yes, attitude is definitely a choice – the right choice for those who seek a successful career. Being optimistic will give you all the strength you need to keep moving successfully toward your goals.

Three things you can do to make
the *attitude* choice:

1 Consciously choose your attitude. Successful people cultivate a habit of positive enthusiasm.

2 Keep your eyes open to new opportunities – even when they come from the most unexpected places. Enjoy the opportunity to succeed.

3 Be easy on yourself and everyone else. We are all works in progress.

"Life is too short not to be happy and too long not to do well."
– Bryan Dodge

The Adversity Choice ...
Conquering
Difficult Times

"Within all of us are wells of thought and dynamos of energy which are not suspected until emergencies arise. Then, oftentimes, we find that it is comparatively simple to double or triple our former capacities and to amaze ourselves by the results achieved."
– Thomas J. Watson

In a recent meeting of twenty highly successful people, the topic of adversity was discussed.

They agreed that overcoming adversity was a critical turning point in their own personal success. But, not until everyone began sharing the adversity they had personally overcome did I realize how universal adversity is.

Within that group, our team had faced cancer, suicide, divorce, loss of children, drug abuse, loss of spouse, significant health issues, bankruptcy and other major areas of disappointments. Everyone there had faced a major crisis.

Successful people have problems just like everyone else. Some of the adversities are beyond anyone's control, and some are self-inflicted. But, regardless of how the adversity arrived, **every successful person has faced, attacked, and conquered adversity somewhere along the way.**

The difference between successful people and average people is that successful people make a conscious choice to spend their energy attacking the problem and moving forward.

Average people choose to spend their energy complaining, justifying and blaming others for the problem, which brings them no closer to a positive outcome. In fact, complaining drains the energy needed to begin working their way through the adversity.

MIRED OR MOTIVATED?

Everyone faces adversity – no one is immune. Adversity is part of life...and every person will be challenged with it at some point.

When adversity invades our lives, that is when we discover what we are made of – and what lies at the core of our character. Our gut-check comes when things go wrong – an unexpected event that hits us squarely between the eyes.

After getting over the adversity shock, we have to make a choice. We can choose to become mired in the quicksand of self-pity – immobilized, stuck and unable to move ahead. Or, we can make the choice to do what is necessary to attack and overcome our adversity.

If asked for examples of people who have attacked and overcome adversity, Lance Armstrong or Christopher Reeve would probably be mentioned often. Both are great examples because they chose to avoid the muck of self-pity and to go on with life and become a voice for many others who were facing similar crises in their lives.

But, look around your organization or circle of friends. You probably don't have to look far to find examples of people who have chosen to attack and conquer their personal adversity. They may not get the national attention, money, or resources like Armstrong or Reeve, but their challenges were just as dramatic.

One of the most positive and enthusiastic people I know is a friend of mine named Melissa. When you meet Melissa, she appears to have it all – a terrific personality, good looks, smart, fun, and successful.

What is not apparent is that Melissa passed a major adversity test that would have destroyed most people. Five years ago, Melissa was a homemaker taking care of her three-year-old autistic child and a newborn – a challenging, full-time job.

One day without warning, Melissa's life suddenly changed. Without any explanation, her husband walked in and said he was leaving. He walked out the door and never turned back, leaving Melissa and the children with the house and the bills … and he moved in with one of Melissa's good friends.

Melissa's world was shattered. Losing her husband and her friend, and being left to pick up the pieces without financial or emotional support was enough to handle. On top of that, she did not have a job because she had left her career four years earlier to stay home and have a family.

Her most logical – and easiest – choice was to become mired in self-pity, bitterness, and hatred over the unfair situation that she was thrown into – who would blame her?

Some say adversity grinds you down. Others say it polishes you up … it depends on what you're made of and how you choose to attack the adversity that comes your way.

Adversity polished Melissa up. She chose to pick up the shattered pieces one at a time and continue to move forward with her life. The trip has been not been easy, but she would not allow adversity to destroy her, her children, or their dreams.

Today, Melissa is a successful graphic designer (she designed this book) and is a tremendous inspiration to me.

Melissa chose to do the best she could with an unfair situation. **Choice is power, and when confronted with adversity, we can choose to see the positive alternatives and rise from the ashes to become even better than we were before – or we can choose to sit and relish in our pitiful circumstances for the rest of our lives.**

CONQUERING ADVERSITY

Chris Novak, my friend and author of *Conquering Adversity* (a book I think every person walking this earth needs to read), is a great example of making the choice to move forward, even after an unimaginable tragedy.

Chris, a happily married family man with one child and another on the way, received a phone call in the middle of just another day at the office, informing him that his wife and unborn son had been killed in an automobile accident. That call would change his life forever. No one would have blamed him for being bitter and consumed with the unfairness of life.

Yet after grieving this tragic loss, Novak chose to take the lessons of catastrophe and create opportunities from the alternatives his life now offered.

In *Conquering Adversity*, he shares how he was able to move forward, saying, "Life is not fair, so don't expect it to be. **Regardless of how bleak the situation appears, there are alternatives that will help you move forward … if you choose to see them.**"

He suggests that you attack adversity by doing the following:

1. **Affirmation** – Acknowledge what is and what is not lost. It is natural in times of extreme duress to believe that everything is lost. We have to acknowledge that, **even in the greatest of tragedies, we do not lose everything.** The fear of moving forward is the power that adversity has over us. Ultimately, we have to make the decision to move ahead.

2. **Expectation** – Adversity attacks our vision, limits our sights and blinds us with the challenges of the moment. After adversity attacks us, we have to make the choice to **pull ourselves up, avoid the "why" trap** and move forward with positive expectations.

3. **Communication** – To conquer adversity, we have to allow others to help. Many times we struggle by ourselves, dealing with adversity when someone just a phone call away would have an answer that would have moved us forward. **People want to help,** but most of the time they have to be invited.

4. **Locomotion** – One of the greatest dangers in facing adversity is that we panic, freeze and stop because we perceive the roadblocks, barriers or mountains in our lives as insurmountable. **People respond better to crisis when they maximize their forward motion.** We have to keep moving forward.

5. **Collaboration** – Most challenges we face cannot be overcome alone. **We should not attempt to meet adversity with no one to support us.** Collaboration is about the people we take with us on our journey forward.

6. **Celebration** – Celebration feeds our positive energy and our sense of hope. **It nourishes our spirits, refreshes our attitudes and gives us strength** to fight off the inevitable attacks of negativism and fear that accompany severe adversity.

Chris Novak's metamorphosis serves as an exquisite model for all of us about how to use catastrophe as a catalyst in our lives. He provides evidence that there are alternatives, even in life's most painful shadows, but Novak is the first to admit that the options for his life became suddenly more plentiful as he began to know himself – for the first time – within the context of his devastating loss.

EXPLORE YOUR ALTERNATIVES

Without question, the better we know ourselves, the more alternatives we can see for our future.

Our personal store of energy, along with our time, is our most valuable commodity. In the face of adversity, we must ask ourselves, "How can my time and energy best be used in this situation right now?"

The obvious answer is, "Exploring workable alternatives – so we can move to the next level."

Making the choice to live life with eyes wide open, even in times of severe adversity, not only makes it possible to consider the alternatives and capture more opportunities, but it also opens us to solutions never before possible and ideas unavailable to closed minds.

Three things you can do to make
the *adversity* choice:

1 Realize that adversity is short-term. Allow others to help you work your way through the adversity you are facing.

2 Don't panic, freeze and stop because you perceive the adversity as insurmountable. People respond better to crisis when you maximize your forward motion. Keep moving forward.

3 Don't waste your energy on looking for someone to blame. Choose to see the positives and opportunities to grow, even in the face of adversity.

"Adversity causes some men to break, others to break records."
– William Arthur Ward

PART THREE

The Investment Choices ...

the profit of success.

Character
1. No-Victim
2. Commitment
3. Values
4. Integrity

Success Choices

Investment
9. Relationship
10. Criticism
11. Reality
12. Legacy

Action
5. Do-Something
6. Persistence
7. Attitude
8. Adversity

"Make every thought, every fact, that comes into your mind pay you a profit. Make it work and produce for you. Think of things not as they are but as they might be. Don't merely dream – but create! "
– Robert Collier

The Relationship Choice ...

Connecting with Success

"Personal relationships are the fertile soil from which all advancement, all success, all achievement in real life grows."
– Ben Stein

Two four-year-olds, both at the stage of discovering that playing alone isn't as much fun as playing with others, began to squabble. Sent to their respective rooms for a thoughtful "time out," the two children were playing together again within 10 minutes, chasing each other and fighting off the bad guys.

For both children, this was one of their first experiences with relationships outside their families – and the learning curve can be painful. However, like most children, the relationship between these two playmates is pliable, able to weather the small tornadoes that come with squabbles and temper tantrums. Once they find it isn't as much fun sitting in a time out as it is playing together, they easily mend their fences and return to enjoying each other's company.

From our earliest experiences as social creatures, our relationships become the palette from which we color and shade our lives, and we're not just talking about our romantic involvements.

BUILDING RELATIONSHIPS

Our relationships – from close family to co-workers, bosses, employees and others with whom we regularly relate – mark our path and are an important part of our lives.

Some of us may have a vast circle of relationships. Others may prefer a more intimate group. Yet the skills in building and maintaining relationships are shared across the spectrum.

But how do we learn to build these relationships? Who teaches us how to develop positive relationships with others?

In some cases, we may have role models within our families or a mentor at work. An older brother or sister may help us pattern our relationships, or perhaps we take our cues from a relative whom we admire and try to emulate, or we may model a person down the hall in the office.

Many of us, however – by choice or necessity – go it alone, relying on our own instincts in creating our own models for building relationships. We take advice from teachers, books, influential associates or larger-than-life heroes on the sports field or the movie screen. Then we put them all together in an enormous collage and use it as a guide for forming and nurturing our relationships.

Sometimes our ideas about what relationships should be – or look like – may be perfectly logical to us but unreasonable to others.

What we seek in healthy relationships for ourselves may be the total opposite of what another would want. Then, too, it is also possible to set up so many requirements for a relationship that no one ever meets the criteria.

The point is this: there is no set pattern, no universal criteria for relationships. Each individual desires and seeks something slightly different.

No matter where your ideas about relationships came from, sooner or later we all discover that **relationships are a requirement for success. You cannot achieve success alone.**

But relationships don't just happen. Healthy, wholesome, energizing relationships take time and energy from both people, and these healthy relationships have a tendency to grow and change over time.

DEVELOPING STABLE RELATIONSHIPS

Researchers have found that the basis for any healthy relationship is trust. Individuals within these relationships also have a willingness to talk through problems, to share openly, and they have developed a comfortable way to share positive and negative feelings with each other.

Individuals in healthy relationships also:

- ♦ Are interested in how other people feel, their concerns and their dreams.
- ♦ Are willing to take responsibility for improving the relationship and encourage other people to do the same.
- ♦ Know that relationships are about more than "what's in it for me?" It's also about what they can bring to the relationship.

♦ Understand that other people not only bring good to experiences but perhaps some negative baggage from other relationships.

♦ Know they impact other people's happiness – and vice versa.

Strangely, in our 21st-century society, when we mention "relationships," meaning our interactions with a broad group of people, most of us take it for granted that a "relationship" is a romantic bond between two people.

In reality, we probably spend less time with our romantic partners than we do with other people ... and we may even spend less time and effort building that romantic relationship than we spend building relationships in the workplace or in other areas of our life.

Strong, positive relationships don't just happen. Oh, yes, a pre-relationship bonding may occur. We may find that perfect chemistry between mentor and student or have an "aha" experience with that individual who shares many of our same interests, but a **strong relationship requires time, attention, understanding and a willingness to see that the needs of the other person are as important as our own.**

It is also true that in our warp-speed society, relationships are sometimes exploited, damaged or forgotten, or they simply run their course, ending abruptly when one of the individuals meets with hardship – a good indicator of those fair-weather friendships formed solely because of the "what's in it for me" motivation.

A BEAR'S ADVICE ON RELATIONSHIPS

As Aesop recalled, two friends were traveling in the woods when a large, hungry bear appeared down the trail. As the bear approached, one of the friends climbed high up in the tree and hid, not offering to help his companion scale the tree. Left with few alternatives, the second friend, who was not as nimble, threw himself on the ground and pretended to be dead, as he had heard that bears would not touch a dead body.

The bear sniffed all around the man on the ground, took him to be dead and went away.

As soon as it was safe, the man came down from the tree and asked his friend what the bear had whispered when he put his mouth to his ear. "He told me to never again travel with a friend who deserts you at the first sign of danger," the survivor replied.

IMPROVING RELATIONSHIPS

Whether the relationship is with your partner, boss, co-workers or friends, there's always room for improvement … so cement those important interactions with more effort on your part. Here are five steps to help cement relationships:

1. Your relationships reflect the relationship you have with yourself. Remember the old saying, "You have to be a friend before you can make friends." So step one is finding peace within yourself. **Take responsibility – nobody can make you happy.** Like that inner peace, it is futile to look elsewhere to find happiness. Treat yourself with caring acceptance and gentle compassion.

2. Everyone wants to know that you care about them. **Show them you care.** Taking a backward glance, think of those who have made you feel special. In most cases, those people made

it obvious to you that they cared about you. No relationship can strengthen and grow in an environment of negativity. Positive thoughts and deeds inspire other people's respect and cause them to value the relationship.

3. We all have busy schedules, but you cannot have a relationship without making time to make contact. **Positive relationships require dedicated time.** Take the time necessary to let the people most important in your life know that you have time for them.

4. Conflicts will occur in any relationship. Be willing to **compromise rather than focusing on winning or losing an argument.** The ultimate test of a relationship is to disagree but to respect, acknowledge the agreement to disagree, and move forward without bitterness.

5. Practice forgiveness when the relationship is tested. **Forgiveness is the "oil" of relationships** … and be prepared for your relationship as well as yourself and the other person to change and evolve with time. Be patient.

Want to expand your circle … increase your opportunities to build new relationships?

There are countless opportunities to meet new people, network and form new relationships. Look around. There are probably numerous people within your work group that you do not know a thing about. The loss is both yours as well as a loss for the people whom you have not taken the time to get to know.

Don't know how to network? Here are a few tips:

1. Decide your interests and join new groups. Going in, be

committed to be involved enough to serve on several committees. Your goal – be the first person the committee remembers when someone asks for help.

2. Go early and stay late. Any class or meeting will have early birds and a "last man (or woman) standing." Meet as many people as you can – and be sure to "work the room" – unless you find someone you're interested in knowing more.

3. Pay attention. If you know people in the group, be sure to ask how projects, event planning, committees or family activities are going.

4. If you say you'll get back with someone or want to follow up, do it. Make contact.

5. Become a mentor for others. Deep relationships are formed when you share the experiences that made you what you are today. People need your counsel, advice and wisdom … don't keep it to yourself.

Social researchers have found that healthy relationships – mutually giving and caring relationships – are a necessity for success. Relationships provide someone to share with, someone to learn from, someone to talk to and someone to confide in. They offer understanding when we fail, solace in our grief and celebration when we continue with our lives.

Relationships are pivotal interactions in enjoying all life has to offer – and key to moving ahead toward success.

Three things you can do to make
the **relationship** choice:

1 Be willing to focus on building positive relationships with your peers, subordinates, friends and boss. Invest time in recognizing your professional relationships. Everyone has a basic need to know they are making a difference. For those making a difference in your life, take the time to write them a note (not e-mail) and express your appreciation for their relationship.

2 Become a mentor for others. People need your counsel, advice, and wisdom … don't keep it to yourself.

3 Don't travel with friends who desert you at the first sign of danger.

"The quality of your life is the quality of your relationships."
– Anthony Robbins

The Criticism Choice ...
Tough Learning

*"Remember, if people talk behind your back,
it only means you're two steps ahead."*
– Fannie Flagg

There's no escaping the fact that success breeds criticism – and the higher people go in their fields, the more susceptible they are to criticism, even if they feel they're doing everything right.

So what is criticism anyway? It is often defined as disapproval expressed by pointing out faults or shortcomings. It is also the judgment of any aspect of other people – how they behave, how they look, how they perform or how they think.

You've probably never met anyone who didn't want to be liked, respected and accepted. In a perfect world, we want everyone to agree with our ideas, and we want our actions to be praised as the best ever. But the reality is that we will have critics ... and having critics is a good thing. Our choice here is about what we do with the criticism that comes our way.

From an early age, we are trained to be critical. Think about your first-grade teacher – the one who wanted you to write a little larger, the one who asked you to read a little louder in reading group, and the one who asked if you would just keep your hands to yourself on the way to the water fountain.

That was criticism – usually very gentle, but firm nonetheless. By the time we were in middle school, the criticism was not only coming from our teachers and parents but also from our peers and perhaps others who didn't even know us.

Successful people have a tendency to attract those who will criticize their every move. In one office I visited recently, it appeared to me as though the corporate culture included back-stabbing and criticizing every single action.

It was like a game. The fast-trackers were criticized for everything, from the way they had their offices arranged to their hairstyles. It was as though the in-house critics were waiting for their next move so they would have something else to discuss critically. Any wonder why turnover was more than 40 percent in that organization?

That type of criticism – criticism focused on your person – will not help you become more successful. Those critics are not worth spending your time on to understand ... instead **find the critics who can help you learn from your mistakes so you can achieve your goals.**

ONE OLD BULLFROG

One warning: Don't overreact to criticism. Those who are critical may be vocal, but alone in their criticism.

There is a story about an old farmer who advertised his "frog farm" for sale. The farm, he claimed, had a pond filled to the brim with fine bullfrogs.

When a prospective buyer appeared, the old farmer asked him to return that evening so he might hear the frogs in full voice. When the buyer returned, he was favorably consumed with the symphony of magical melodies emanating from the pond, and he signed the bill of sale on the spot.

A few weeks later, the new owner decided to drain the pond so that he could catch and market the plentiful supply of frogs – but to his amazement, when the water was drained from the pond, he found that all the noise had been made by one old bullfrog.

The same may also be said about criticism in an organization. Usually, the most noise is made by only one old bullfrog.

CHOOSING TO EMBRACE CRITICISM

So why would we want to choose criticism?

Ultimately, **we all need criticism, no matter how successful we become.** Criticism whips our fragmented attention into laser focus on some of the more important aspects of our jobs and our lives. Some call criticism a "teaching tool." More specifically, it is a learning tool that teaches us hard lessons throughout our lives.

Unlike the way that many people think, criticism isn't always negative. In fact, in many forums, criticism is a positive, necessary part of growth.

If we examine our own criticisms of others, we'll discover that we use our own narrow standards to judge others – from spouses to houses. Obviously, for criticism to be meaningful, the better path is to be more flexible and less judgmental when we look at others and their actions. Just because we wouldn't have done it the same way doesn't mean another's approach doesn't have merit – and perhaps more than our own approach.

The healthy approach to criticism is to pay attention to it. Always listen with the intent to understand – why the criticism is being leveled at you and why the critic may want you to know his or her feelings.

You see, there's an upside to criticism, too. Criticism from the right people could lead to improvement. Many employees dread performance reviews. They know that criticism is on the way, even though there are probably more positives than negatives in performance reviews. The people who pay attention to the feedback and make adjustments based on it are the ones who will ultimately get the next promotion.

The biggest room we have is the room for improvement. There's always something we can do better, more often or with a different intensity. **Appropriate criticism helps us focus our attention on what we need to do to become more successful.**

AVOIDING PSYCHOSCLEROSIS

We've all heard people say, "I welcome constructive criticism," but sometimes that invitation is hard to believe.

Why? Because of our human nature, constructive criticism carries a certain sting, even though it may help us correct a wrong, strengthen a weakness or chart a more successful course. One reason for criticism's stinging effect is something referred to as psychosclerosis, our natural tendency to think that our idea is the best – or the only – idea that will work.

The second phase of full-blown psychosclerosis is becoming closed-minded to any suggestion. So if we think we have the best or only idea and we're closed to any suggestions, the result is that we become stagnated in our own stubbornness.

The opposite of psychosclerosis is the ability to be flexible – listening with the intent to learn so that you can make a better-educated decision.

So once you make the "criticism choice," what's the best way to handle criticism – from your colleagues, your boss, your friends or your partner? Here are a few suggestions:

1. Acknowledge that **criticism is a form of feedback** – and we all need feedback.

2. Ask yourself these questions: Who's offering the criticism – is he or she qualified? **Is he or she trying to hurt you, or is he or she trying to help?** Objectively, is there any truth to what he or she is saying?

3. **Constructive criticism is a gift.** Thank the giver.

4. Be willing to learn from what's been said. **Don't put your self-esteem at the mercy of others.** Liking who you are makes it easier to evaluate the criticism of others.

5. Attempt to transform criticism that seems directed at your "person" to specific behavioral issues. Criticism, when directed at one's "person," may weaken one's resolve. **Focus the criticism on your actions … not your person.** Pay particularly close attention to criticism that addresses behaviors and is timely and specific.

6. After you have a chance to review the criticism, communicate clearly how you feel and think about the criticism: then **take appropriate action to improve.**

7. If you want constructive criticism from others (and you should), **be willing to return the favor if they are interested.**

Criticism is a fact of life. You have the choice to perceive criticism as a hindrance or a help. Experts in human behavior encourage us to be prepared to accept criticism and to accept it graciously.

Realistically, criticism – both constructive criticism and criticism that is less so – should eventually become a tool with which we grow as individuals while evolving our skills and our ideas. Ultimately, we can find the comfort zone – the fine line between dismissing criticism and clinging to each word we hear – and welcome criticism rather than become defensive when criticism comes our way.

Three things you can do to make
the *criticism* choice:

1 Be aware that criticism comes with success. Embrace it and learn from it.

2 Accept constructive criticism as a gift. It can enlighten you to the changes you need to make to be successful.

3 Acknowledge that criticism is a learning tool that teaches us lessons throughout our lives.

"Criticism is the windows and chandeliers of art: it illuminates the enveloping darkness in which art might otherwise rest only vaguely discernible, and perhaps altogether unseen."
– George Jean Nathan

The Reality Choice ...
Facing Truth

"Face reality as it is ... not as you wish it to be."
– Jack Welch, former CEO of GE

Carmen Silva had worked for years to reach her position as a manager for a large corporation. Yet as she watched colleagues move ahead in their careers, the reality was that her own career was being slowed because of her long-standing fear about speaking in front of groups.

* * *

Nick Bagby made his quota every month. He had won every award for productivity and had even earned several trips to Hawaii as leading sales rep for his division, but he had been passed over for sales manager promotions for the past three years. In his place, two colleagues had gone on to higher positions.

"Nothing personal, Nick," his boss had said, trying to reassure him. "The reality is that since your kids are in school, you've never wanted to relocate your family – and we haven't had openings here in over five years."

* * *

Carl Landon had been a top-notch office manager for a large corporation for several years, but he had always wanted to go into sales. However, every time he had approached the VP of sales about the possibilities of joining the sales force, he had been less than encouraged. Finally, he confronted the VP. "What's wrong with me becoming a sales rep?" he wanted to know.

"Frankly, Carl," the VP responded, "I just don't think that job is right for you. It requires a lot of self-motivation to succeed in sales, and, as we've discussed in the past, self-motivation is just not something you've demonstrated in your current assignment."

The reality: Carl had been "interviewing" all along. His skills and personality were better suited to a structured environment.

* * *

History chronicles our preference to avoid facing reality. In 1775, American patriot Patrick Henry spoke of this preference to the Continental Congress about the British intent to subjugate the colonies:

> *"We are apt to shut our eyes against a painful truth,*
> *and listen to the song of that siren till she transforms*
> *us into beasts. Are we disposed to be of the number of*

those who, having eyes, see not, and, having ears, hear
not, the things which so nearly concern their temporal
salvation? For my part, whatever anguish of spirit it
may cost, I am willing to know the whole truth; to
know the worst, and to provide for it."

All too often, when we suddenly find ourselves facing reality, it's not a reality we want to see.

In Carl's case, as an example, he wanted to try his luck, to see if he could perform as well as – or better than – the current sales reps. He thought he had the personality, thought he knew the products. All he needed was a chance, but the reality was that the current VP wasn't too impressed with the way Carl handled slack times – times top sales reps spent developing leads and making cold calls. Apparently the VP couldn't envision Carl performing without a specific routine, one that had built-in accountability at every turn. Carl failed to realize that he was interviewing for his next opportunity while working his current job.

THE TRUTH OF REALITY

A definition of the word *reality* tells us it is the real nature of something; the truth or something that is actual, not imaginary.

A key element to your success will be discovering and facing reality. The process of discovering reality includes examining the facts and separating them from our feelings and egos.

"So why is the choice of reality necessary for a successful life journey?" you may be asking.

We choose reality and use it as a springboard to our next goal-setting process. We choose reality as a tool to understand what's in front of us – from the opportunities along our path to the challenges that loom ahead.

Choosing reality provides us with a major indicator about where we are, where we're going and what we have to do to get there.

Like visiting a large mall and searching for the map of stores so we can locate the nearest coffee shop or optician, choosing reality tells us, "You are here." Then, using the map as a guide to where we want to go next, reality allows us to plot our path to get from where we are to where we want to go.

Choosing reality also helps us make those difficult decisions … when the VP of sales pointed out that Carl, the office manager who wanted to be a sales rep, didn't always use his slack time productively, the reality of that message provided Carl with three options – he could keep being an office manager, he could learn to use his slack time wisely, or he could go to another company, make a fresh start and demonstrate just how productive he could be.

Reality also can help identify our limits. During the last several seasons of his career, former Dallas Cowboys quarterback Troy Aikman was warned by his doctors that repeated concussions had placed him in a precarious position every time he walked onto the playing field. He had the ability to continue to be a great quarterback, but it could take only one more crushing, jarring tackle to place his life in jeopardy. For Aikman, the reality soon became that continuing his football career could cost him his life.

In business, the limits of reality can come in the form of our abilities, our product, our leadership or even the capitalization of a company or the wishes of stockholders. In the last decade, the reality of downsizing meant that many in the workforce had to retool their skills and enter other industries.

The old phrase – time for a reality check – is exactly the approach workers should take in assessing where they are (as in "You are here") and where they want to be or where they want to go.

Reality, for most of us, means change – a change in our plans or our dreams, a change in our direction, a change in our approach to solving a problem or a change in our team.

STOPPING FOR A REALITY CHECK

All too often, we don't stop long enough for a "reality check" and keep going as long as we can, before there are no other options. Like so many of us, we're in such a hurry with such a busy schedule that we don't take time to stop to refill the fuel tank – until we're on the freeway at six in the evening and we're praying we can make it to a gas station before our vehicle sputters to a stop.

Choosing reality can help us avoid those awkward moments, whether it's running out of fuel on the freeway or sitting across the desk during an exit interview with a favorite employee. Choosing reality can mean sizing up what it takes to clear the hurdle ahead of us before taking the next giant step in our careers or, like Troy Aikman, understanding that making changes now may be our best option.

But **choosing reality does not mean abandoning lofty goals and dreams. In fact, it's just the opposite.** Being realistic provides you with the best chance of attaining those dreams because reality keeps giving accurate and objective assessments of what you need to reach success.

In 1994, a popular movie called *Reality Bites* appeared in theatres around the country. The premise involved the realities of the lives of Gen-Xers as they transitioned from college to careers.

Whether you liked this movie or not, the message carried by the title sums up the negative aspects that being realistic often offers. Sure, it "bites" when you suddenly find yourself in a job you don't like or your company is struggling.

Reality "bites" when your partner no longer wants to share your life, when you can no longer afford a certain lifestyle, or when you find that your first-born has been sneaking out of the house after you're asleep.

Yes, choosing reality can often lead you down a murky path where you may refuse to speak of the unspeakable or think the unthinkable. But by choosing reality, you're taking the first step in solving the problem or ending a situation that is not only disturbing to you but also probably sapping your emotional energy.

REALITY REWARDS
Are there rewards for confronting these hard realities?

Absolutely: Of course, you should prepare yourself to encounter frequent delays in your forward progress, as well as bouts of self-doubt and pessimism. However, as you make the reality choice – the best and the worst – you are not only rewarded by learning more about yourself, but you also will find that – in dealing with obstacle after obstacle – you can use many of these challenges to your advantage.

In discussing the necessary traits of future business leaders, Harvard's Ronald Heifetz said **tomorrow's greatest leaders are those with the courage to face reality and help the people around them face reality**. In doing so, the vision of that organization becomes accurate, and strategies can be developed to achieve what's possible with this authentic vision.

As an example, as you plot your plan for the next year or set your goals for the next five years, some of the realities you will assess are the skills, time, resources and motivation needed to reach those goals – and whether there is a gap between these resources and what your goals demand for success.

Choosing reality takes courage … it takes strength of conviction and a passion for progress. All too often, we'd be much more comfortable kicking reality under the carpet as we stand and admire our last award-winning project.

But if we choose reality and all this choice entails, we will find the road to success a little straighter, the challenges less overwhelming, our goals within reach, and fewer surprises along the way.

Three things you can do to make
the *reality* choice:

1. A key element of your success is discovering and facing reality. Reality is actual, not imaginary. Make reality checks a daily habit.

2. Look for truth – in every situation, every relationship, every crisis and every success. Reality checks will help you identify your limits and allow you to focus on your opportunities.

3. Understand that choosing reality may not always be the easiest path, but, bottom line, it will push us ahead on the road of life.

"Either you deal with what is the reality,
or you can be sure that the reality is going to deal with you."
– Alex Haley

The Legacy Choice ...
Your Gift

"In everyone's life, at some time, our inner fire goes out. It is then burst into flame by an encounter with another human being. We should all be thankful for those people who rekindle the inner spirit."
– Albert Schweitzer

Jim Spier has been giving of himself through the Boy Scouts for many years. Drawing from personal experience, he provides this interesting insight: In your mind's eye, take a look at any 100 boys who have recently joined Scouting:

- Of those 100 boys, rarely will one ever appear before a juvenile court.

- Twelve of the 100 will receive their first religious contact through Scouting.

- Eighteen will develop hobbies and interests that will last all their lives.

- Eight will find their future vocation through badge work and Scouting contacts.

- One will use Scouting skills to save another person's life, and one will be credited with saving his own life.

- Seventeen will become future Scout leaders and will give leadership to additional thousands of boys.

For the sake of comparison, according to the Justice Department's Report on Juvenile Crime (Washington, D.C., U.S. Government Printing Office, 2002), there were 2.3 million juvenile arrests in the United States in 2001.

Of that group, 1,400 were arrested for murder. Approximately 500,000 arrests were made for burglary, theft, auto theft and arson. More than 105,000 youth were arrested for vandalism, 37,500 were arrested for carrying weapons, and 202,500 were arrested on illegal drug charges.

What is the difference between the Scouts and the arrested juveniles? Of course, many factors could come into play, but one obvious difference is that the Scouts have someone guiding them – a mentor providing light through the pitch-black darkness of making choices.

The choice of legacy, whether it be as a Boy or Girl Scout leader, a business mentor, a teacher, or a volunteer consultant, is an important choice – a necessary choice for you to achieve success.

Moreover, without people choosing the legacy choice, our society would be stymied. There would be no positive role models, no examples, no endowments, no helping hands, no help for the homeless, and no voice for the voiceless.

Think back to your own childhood. Without too much effort, you can probably not only name an adult mentor, outside your family, who left an imprint on your life – but you can also probably envision that person's face or a specific activity.

In most cases, these important individuals were passionate about their mission, whether it was showing you the ropes in your first job or showing you how to dribble a basketball in elementary school. They not only knew the importance of giving of themselves, but they also saw you as an important recipient of their gifts.

GETTING THE COLD, HARD – AND VALUABLE – FACTS

When I first began my business, I went to visit Fred Smith, an author and mentor to many successful businesspeople in Dallas. He is probably one of the wisest men I've ever met. But his approach to mentoring sessions was far from coddling me, the neophyte. Instead, he was brutal with me as he provided me with information that was honest and which I value, even today, as some of the most important information I would hear. He painted no pretty pictures, served up no pie in the sky. Instead, he immediately seized my attention and told me not only how it was going to be but how to avoid certain obstacles in the future as well as some I wouldn't be able to avoid.

The times I spent with Fred Smith have provided me with more information and more momentum than any college degree, any experience in the field.

More than once in my own presentations and in my books, I have referred to Fred's guidance. It is his legacy, one I value more than words can express.

But what would happen if there were no willing mentors – like Fred Smith or Jim Spier?

Think about it. Without mentors, we would not have the wealth of past experience to call upon, the wisdom to look beyond the horizon for the next strategy or direction. Without willing volunteers, how many thousands of children and young adults would go without exposure to quality individuals with something to share?

Many successful men and women hold in common the choice to leave behind a legacy that will live on long after their last breaths.

But how do we – in this day and time – really feel about this legacy of giving?

Are we put here to give a bit of ourselves to others? Are we defined by what we give?

Why should we choose to give? It takes a lot of endurance to put other people first, particularly when they're often so preoccupied with themselves that they don't seem to notice our efforts. And, our schedules are normally full, even before we start giving our time and energy to others.

We should choose to give because it is the right thing to do.

PEOPLE AND PEANUTS

George Washington Carver not only knew something about peanuts, but he was also intimately familiar with the human condition. He understood the importance of legacy, of giving to others, when he said, "How far you go in life depends on you being tender with the young, compassionate with the aged, sympathetic with the striving and tolerant of the weak and the strong. Because someday in life you will have been all of these."

When asked about giving of ourselves, another wise sage counseled, "Don't expect the people you help to be there to help you when you're in need yourself."

Excellent advice! The purpose of giving is not to receive back in full measure. If you give solely with the expectation of receiving something in return, prepare to be disappointed. After all, if expecting something in return is your reason for giving, you are really not giving – you're swapping. If you receive something in return of your gift, what you receive is a bonus – not a repayment of debt.

The joy of your legacy is in the gift you give, not in what you receive in return. You legacy cannot be taken with you … that's why there are no luggage racks on hearses.

When you put someone else first, your gift smoothes off the rough edges that make human relationships difficult. You're rounding off the corners that have prevented the square pegs from fitting into society's round holes. But don't expect a thank-you note or a pat on the head. Choose to give because it is the right thing to do.

BEGIN YOUR LEGACY WHERE YOU ARE

Some attempt to sidestep giving of themselves by saying, "I wouldn't know where to start – or what to give."

Giving back can be as simple as working overtime so another employee can attend her daughter's soccer game. It can be manning the phones during a telethon or speaking to a group of students at career day. **Only your time and wisdom are required to build a legacy.**

Seneca, the ancient Roman philosopher, anticipated this hesitancy of knowing where to start. "Where there is another human being," he wrote, "there is always an opportunity for kindness."

Start with the person who sits next to you at work – your peer, your boss or just an acquaintance. Start somewhere. You never know where you will make a difference that will change a person's life.

THE UNREACHABLE STUDENT

At the end of the semester, a college professor was looking over her students as they took the final examination. Her eyes encountered one student – a young woman – who seemed too absorbed in things outside the classroom to ever make much of a contribution. The professor shook her head, feeling as though she had not done enough to reach the girl. It was rare that she didn't share successes with her students.

At the end of the final examination, the young woman placed her exam on the professor's desk and handed her an envelope. On its front, the student had taped two candy canes. Inside was a holiday card with the usual message … but beneath the printed message, the student had written the following:

> *Thank you for making me feel – for the first time – that my ideas were important and that I had something of value, something to contribute to your class. I will never forget you.*

Don't judge the impact of your legacy solely on the outward response of those around you. Many times, when we are least aware, a gesture, an encouraging word or a smile will encourage others more than we'll ever know.

THE LAW OF LEGACY

Essentially, **giving of ourselves should come from the heart – and, without fail, when this kind of giving happens, we are generously repaid for every kindness we share.**

There is a legendary story about a farmer who discovered a young boy stuck in a mud bog somewhere in the United Kingdom. After much struggle, the farmer was finally able to free the lad, although for a moment the farmer felt that he, too, would sink too deeply into the mud to survive. Later that evening, a lord stopped by the farmer's humble shanty, identifying himself as the rescued boy's father and offering to pay him a generous reward for his effort.

When the farmer refused, the lord saw that the farmer had a son and insisted that he pay the boy's way to college. After he graduated with a degree in science, the young man – Alexander Fleming – went on to discover penicillin. Ironically, the young man who had been rescued from the bog, now a young adult, came down with pneumonia. Thanks to Fleming's discovery – penicillin – his life was saved. The young man's name: Sir Winston Churchill.

Whether this tale is true or a mix of myth and legend, its moral easily reflects life – what we do for others eventually comes back to us multiplied. It's the law of legacy.

TRUSTED MENTORS LEAVE THEIR MARKS

Most successful people have the luxury of a mentor. Maybe for you it was a grandparent, teacher or colleague … someone to provide sound advice while you were blazing a career or personal path foreign to you. That mentor was able to clear the fog from your vision.

For Mitch Albom, a terrific writer, his mentor was Morrie Schwartz … his college professor. For 20 years or so, Mitch lost track of Morrie, as his career was consuming all of his time and energy.

Mitch rediscovered Morrie in Morrie's last months of life. Knowing that Morrie was dying, they began meeting every Tuesday, and Morrie shared his life lessons with Mitch. The result was a wonderful book, *Tuesdays With Morrie.*

Morrie left a lasting legacy through his time with Mitch, and Mitch's gift and legacy were writing *Tuesdays With Morrie,* which allows all of us to learn from a wise mentor.

MENTORING – SHARING THE WAY OUT

Once there was a man walking down the street who fell into a hole. The hole was so deep he could not escape. He looked in all directions and could not figure out how to raise himself from the hole.

A preacher walked by, heard the man's cry for help and inquired, "Why are you in that hole in the road?" The man replied: "I fell in and I can't get out." The preacher said that he would pray for him and walked away.

A police officer walked by, heard the man's cry for help and inquired,

"Why are you in that hole in the road?" The man replied: "I fell in and I can't get out." The policeman said it was against the law to be in a hole in the road, wrote him a ticket, threw it into the hole and walked away.

An environmentalist walked by, heard the man's cry for help and inquired, "Why are you in that hole in the road?" The man replied, "I fell in and I can't get out." The environmentalist said it was environmentally unsafe to be in a hole in the road and began to picket, circling the hole and holding a sign reading, "Man in Hole in Road … Environmentally Unsafe!"

A friend walked by, heard the man's cry for help and inquired, "Why are you in that hole in the road?" The man replied, "I fell in and I can't get out." Without hesitation, the friend jumped into the hole with him.

The man in the hole said, "Why did you jump in this hole? I can't get out. I have had preachers praying for me, police writing me a ticket, and this goofy person picketing outside. And you chose to jump down here with me. Are you crazy? Why would you jump down here with me?"

The friend replied, "Don't worry. I chose to jump in this hole with you because I have been in this hole before, and I know the way out!"

Maybe you have not faced a situation that has led to someone being in a "deep hole." Nevertheless, you can listen to, coach and support those who are working their way out of the holes they have fallen into.

Trusted counselors, mentors and guides make an indelible mark on the lives they touch, and they provide the two ingredients to success in life – caring and sharing – that cannot be learned or purchased.

What is your legacy? What marks are you leaving along the path for the next generation?

We leave our legacies by choice. No one requires us to make this contribution. It is something we do to help someone along the way, to support our colleagues, our friends and those whom we may not know. It is a gift that comes without a price tag. Your legacy is priceless.

You may be successful, but your choice to leave a legacy by giving of yourself distinguishes you most, providing the greatest meaning to your life because your example will live into the next generation through the lives you touch.

Three things you can do to make
the *legacy* choice:

1 Be willing to share what you know, and mentor those looking for the pathway to success.

2 The greatest gift you can give is your knowledge and experiences. Giving of ourselves should come from the heart – and without fail, when this kind of giving happens, we are generously repaid for every kindness we share.

3 Begin your legacy where you are – there's always an opportunity for others to learn from you.

"We must give more in order to get more. It is the generous giving of ourselves that produces the generous harvest."
– Orison Swett Marden

The Final Word

Preparing for that special moment of success

~

"To every man there comes in his lifetime **that special moment** *when he is tapped on the shoulder and offered the chance to do a very special thing. What a tragedy if that moment finds him unprepared or unqualified for the work which would be his finest hour."*
– Winston Churchill

This book was written to help you prepare for your special moment of success.

Andrew Carnegie once said, "The average person puts only 25 percent of his energy and ability into his work. The world takes off its hat to those who put in more than 50 percent of their capacity and stands on its head for those few and far between souls who devote 100 percent."

What a shame!

You have too much talent to be average. I hope you will make the choice to be one of the few-and-far-between souls who give everything they have to become successful.

Becoming successful is hard work, and, like a business, it must be budgeted. The business budget is the plan for expenditures, appropriate allocation of resources, and accounting of results. The budget must be somewhat fluid, as adjustments have to be made to account for changing conditions.

Planning your career success is the same – plan where you will expend your time and energy, focus on the important activities that help you accomplish your plan, and hold yourself accountable for success.

Your success is increasing or decreasing in value every day based on your choices. Most of the time, it is not just one choice that separates the successful from those who fall short of success. It is an accumulation of many choices that make the difference.

My desire is that the information shared in this book will motivate you to make the choices necessary for you to become the very best at your chosen profession.

May life's journey bring you good choices, success and prosperity!

12 Choices – 12 Questions

The Character Choices ...

1. **The no-victim choice** – don't let your past eat your future.
   Do I accept total responsibility for my success?

2. **The commitment choice** – passionate enough to succeed.
   Am I committed to paying the price of success?

3. **The values choice** – choosing the right enemies.
   Do I accept that there will be enemies who oppose my values and success?

4. **The integrity choice** – doing the right thing.
   Will my success be accomplished without sacrificing my integrity?

The Action Choices ...

5. **The do-something choice** ... don't vacation on Someday Isle.
   Will I attack complacency and do something daily that will move me toward success?

6. **The persistence choice** ... learning from failure.
   Will I hang in there ... beyond failure ... long enough to achieve success?

7. **The attitude choice** ... the enthusiastic approach.
   Will I take a positive and enthusiastic approach to the unexpected twists and turns of life?

8. **The adversity choice** … conquering difficult times.

Will I work through adversity and achieve my goals regardless of the unfair and difficult things that may happen along the way?

The Investment Choices …

9. **The relationship choice** … connecting with success.

Will I invest time in building positive relationships with my peers, family and friends?

10. **The criticism choice** … tough learning.

Do I accept criticism as valuable feedback that will help me achieve success?

11. **The reality choice** … facing truth.

Am I true to myself and all those around me?

12. **The legacy choice** … your gift.

Do I share my gift of experience and knowledge with others?

The Final Question:

Am I prepared for my special moment of success?

12 Choices – 12 Questions Reminder Card
(Laminated, Pocket-sized)
is available at
www.cornerstoneleadership.com

ACKNOWLEDGEMENTS

Over the years, I have been one of the most fortunate people in the world because of my family, friends, and associates. My success has been molded and formed by those with whom I have been fortunate enough to be on the same team.

Thanks to my family, who has been my inspiration:

My wife, Karen, who made the adversity choice to fight and win her battle with cancer and now is a positive role model for many others facing the battle for their lives.

My daughter Jennifer, who made the choice to persist and work her way through the traps that so many young adults fall victim to.

My daughter Kim, who made the choice of doing something and becoming the most supportive, positive and loving daughter anyone could ask for.

And, my son, Michael, who made the attitude choice of living his life in a positive, enthusiastic manner regardless of any challenge he may be facing.

Thanks to my friends who have been my encouragement: Ken Carnes, Lee Colan, Ty Deleon, Logan Garrett, Eric Harvey, Louis Kruger, Mark Layton, Joe Miles, Tod Taylor, and many others have helped me through the good times and the times when adversity seemed overwhelming.

Thanks to the CornerStone team that has been the reason for my success: Juli Baldwin, Barbara Bartlett, Ken Carnes, Melissa Monogue, Sue Coffman, Lee Colan, Billy Cox, Bryan Dodge, Jim Garner, Harry Hopkins, Tony Jeary, Shawn Kirwan, Stephen Krempl, Chris Novak, Vince Poscente, David Reed, and Valerie Sokolosky.

And, especially Alice Adams, who made her legacy choice eight years ago by mentoring and providing me her knowledge and expertise on how to write books.

To each person who reads this book, best wishes as you make the right choices for you to accomplish the success you deserve.

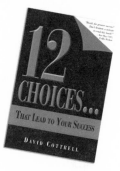

Six ways to bring the
12 Choices ...
That Lead to Your Success
message to your team:

1. *12 Choices PowerPoint® Presentation*
Introduce and reinforce the 12 Choices to your organization with this complete and cost-effective companion presentation piece. All the main concepts and ideas in the book are reinforced in this professionally produced, downloadable **PowerPoint presentation with facilitator guide and notes.** Use the presentation for kick-off meetings, training sessions or as a follow-up development tool. **$79.95**

2. *Keynote Presentation*
Invite author David Cottrell to inspire your team to make better choices and create success for your organization. Each presentation is designed to set a solid foundation for both organizational and personal success.

3. *12 Choices Success Workshop*
Facilitated by David Cottrell or a certified CornerStone Leadership instructor, this three or six hour workshop will reinforce the principles of *12 Choices*. Each person will develop a personal plan that will make a profound difference in their life and career.

4. *12 Choices Personal Profile*
This online profile assesses your personal strengths and provides insight to gaps or blind spots that may prevent your success. It provides the framework to create an actionable development plan leveraging the Character, Action and Investment choices.

5. *12 Choices ... That Lead to Your Success* Audio CD   **$19.95**

6. *12 Choices – 12 Questions* Reminder Card
Pocket-sized, laminated. **Pk/20 $19.95**

www.cornerstoneleadership.com   **1.888.789.LEAD**

Recommended Reading:

You and Your Network is profitable reading for those who want to learn how to develop healthy relationships with others. **$9.95**

Becoming the Obvious Choice is a roadmap showing employees how they can maintain their motivation, develop their hidden talents, and become the best. **$9.95**

Leadership ER is a powerful story that shares valuable insights on how to achieve and maintain personal health, business health and the critical balance between the two. Read it and develop your own prescription for personal and professional health and vitality. **$14.95**

You Gotta Get in the Game...Playing to Win in Business, Sales and Life provides direction on how to get into and win the game of life and business. **$14.95**

Conquering Adversity...Six Strategies to Move You and Your Team Through Tough Times is practical guide to help people and organizations deal with the unexpected and move forward through adversity. **$14.95**

175 Ways to Get More Done in Less Time has 175 really good suggestions that will help you get things done faster...usually better. **$9.95**

The Ant and the Elephant is a different kind of book for a different kind of leader! A great story that teaches that we must lead ourselves before we can expect to be an effective leader of others. **$12.95**

Monday Morning Leadership is David Cottrell's best-selling book. It offers unique encouragement and direction that will help you become a better manager, employee, and person. **$12.95**

136 Effective Presentation Tips is a powerful handbook providing 136 practical, easy-to-use tips to make every presentation a success. **$9.95**

Visit www.**cornerstoneleadership**.com
for additional books and resources.

☑ YES! Please send me extra copies of *12 Choices ... That Lead to Your Success!*

1-30 copies $14.95   31-100 copies $13.95   100+ copies $12.95

12 Choices ... That Lead to Your Success	____ copies X _____	= $ _____
12 Choices Audio CD	____ copies X $19.95	= $ _____
12 Choices Reminder Card (pocket-sized/laminated)	____ pk/20 X $19.95	= $ _____

Additional Leadership Development Resources

You and Your Network	____ copies X $9.95	= $ _____
Becoming the Obvious Choice	____ copies X $9.95	= $ _____
Leadership ER	____ copies X $14.95	= $ _____
You Gotta Get in the Game	____ copies X $14.95	= $ _____
Conquering Adversity	____ copies X $14.95	= $ _____
175 Ways to Get More Done in Less Time	____ copies X $9.95	= $ _____
The Ant and the Elephant	____ copies X $12.95	= $ _____
Monday Morning Leadership	____ copies X $12.95	= $ _____
136 Effective Presentation Tips	____ copies X $9.95	= $ _____
12 Choices Package (Includes all of the items listed above, except the Reminder Card.)	____ packs X $119.95	= $ _____
	Shipping & Handling	$ _____
	Subtotal	$ _____
	Sales Tax (8.25%-TX Only)	$ _____
	Total (U.S. Dollars Only)	$ _____

Shipping and Handling Charges

Total $ Amount	Up to $49	$50-$99	$100-$249	$250-$1199	$1200-$2999	$3000+
Charge	$6	$9	$16	$30	$80	$125

Name _____ Job Title _____

Organization _____ Phone _____

Shipping Address _____ Fax _____

Billing Address _____ Email _____

City _____ State _____ Zip _____

❑ Please invoice (Orders over $200) Purchase Order Number (if applicable) _____

Charge Your Order: ❑ MasterCard   ❑ Visa   ❑ American Express

Credit Card Number _____ Exp. Date _____

Signature _____

❑ Check Enclosed (Payable to CornerStone Leadership)

Fax	Mail	Phone
972.274.2884	**P.O. Box 764087** **Dallas, TX 75376**	**888.789.5323**

www.**cornerstoneleadership**.com

CornerStone
Leadership Institute